Betty Smith, in *Be*_ again succeeds in taking us with her on an amazing journey, interspersing anecdote with instruction as she uses her own life as a testimony to the enduring and inestimable love of God. Having been blessed by her friendship, I encourage you to sit back and let her fill your heart with the profound peace and joy of knowing Jesus Christ as Savior. Lord...and best Friend.

Betty speaks to new seekers of faith along with "veteran believers" with her loving and encouraging message that throughout all, we have a God who loves us deeply, Who keeps his promises to us, opens doors and sustains us, comforts us, delights us, and sends us angels along with laughter and joy. In all, numerous passages of scripture reinforce the powerful lessons offered here. I often found myself stopping to pray as I read certain passages, remembering to give thanks for a wonderful time or to lift up a friend in need of prayer...or even to be reminded of a favorite passage I had not thought of in a while. In between, we get to share vicariously with Betty and her family as they experience ups and downs (and a lot of laughs) on mission in Mexico and a wonderful trip to Italy.

If you have been fortunate enough to hear Betty speak, you will hear her voice in the words on the page. Betty writes as she speaks, with gentleness, clarity, humor, and an unmistakable love for Jesus. You may shed tears as she touches your heart or laugh out loud at her comments, but when you finish her narrative, you will feel just fine about being a "cracked pot" because more of God's love can shine through. Reader, may you be blessed!

—CASSANDRA RACE, PHD
SOUTHERN POLYTECHNIC STATE UNIVERSITY
MARIETTA, GEORGIA

Nestled among Betty Smith's wonderful testimony and various life experiences are found deep, insightful Bible lessons. This book is inspiring, educational, entertaining, and touching. I was truly blessed and encouraged by Betty's book, and I plan to recommend it to all my friends and family.

—EVELYN WELLS
ST. PAUL UNITED METHODIST CHURCH
GAINESVILLE, GEORGIA

Betty Smith's wonderful new book, *Beyond the Happy Ending*, is a winning combination that offers an opportunity to build a foundation of challenging passages from Genesis to Revelation. It gives a relevant and rich devotional Gospel resource for any individual.

—REVEREND ROOSEVELT WINFREY, JR.
SENIOR PASTOR
EAST POINT PRESBYTERIAN CHURCH
EAST POINT, GEORGIA

BEYOND

THE

Happy Ending

BETTY T. SMITH

BEYOND
THE
Happy Ending

CREATION
HOUSE

BEYOND THE HAPPY ENDING by Betty Smith
Published by Creation House
A Charisma Media Company
600 Rinehart Road
Lake Mary, Florida 32746
www.charismamedia.com

Unless otherwise noted, all Scripture quotations are from King James
Version of the Bible.

Scripture quotations marked NKJV are from the New King James Version of
the Bible. Copyright © 1979, 1980, 1982 by Thomas Nelson, Inc., publishers.
Used by permission.

Scripture quotations marked THE MESSAGE are from The Message: The
Bible in Contemporary English, copyright © 1993, 1994, 1995, 1996, 2000,
2001, 2002. Used by permission of NavPress Publishing Group.

Names of persons included in this book have been changed to preserve
their privacy.

Design Director: Bill Johnson
Cover design by Nathan Morgan

Visit the author's website: www.bettyterrysmith.com

Library of Congress Cataloging-in-Publication Data: 2011932338
International Standard Book Number: 978-1-61638-648-1
E-book ISBN: 978-1-61638-649-8
While the author has made every effort to provide accurate telephone
numbers and Internet addresses at the time of publication, neither the
publisher nor the author assumes any responsibility for errors or for
changes that occur after publication.

First edition

11 12 13 14 15 — 987654321
Printed in Canada

Acknowledgments

I THANK THE FOLLOWING partners and promoters in this amazing journey:

My "Back to Basics" Sunday school class, who love to dig with me into the Word of God and take rabbit trails;

My sisters of "Common Bonds," who listen and love me (and chocolate);

Jane Gunter, Director of Family Life Ministries, and all the volunteers, who are "Jesus-with-skin-on" to His wounded ones, and who graciously allow me to serve with them;

Jill Growney, my very own personal editor and Number One Encourager; and

The team at Creation House, who once again nurtured my dream and brought it to fruition.

May the seed you have invested in me be returned to you at least a thousand times over and beyond!

Dedication

To the Glory of the Father, Son, and Holy Spirit. You have accepted me in the beloved and continue to take me beyond my wildest dreams!

Table of Contents

Introduction

I F YOU HAD asked me, a young girl growing up in the South in the Forties, what was my goal in life, I would have happily answered that I wanted to be a wife and mother. There was a popular television show at that time called *My Three Sons*, so the picture in my head was a handsome husband and three equally handsome boys. My dream began to be fulfilled on June 29, 1952, when I married my high school sweetheart, Bob.

Having children was not so easily accomplished, but the Lord heard my pleas, and on April 17, 1959, our first son, Steve, graced our lives. More time passed, and on May 17, 1964, our second son, Scott, entered our world with a bang; he was in a hurry to arrive! Just one more son and my dream would be complete.

A woman has the prerogative to change her mind, or perhaps the Lord was turning my heart. I prayed, placing my hands on my pregnant tummy, that if it would fit into His scheme of things, I would love to have a daughter. Stacey Elizabeth became a member of our family on November 8, 1965. Apparently, He thought it was just fine!

We had been married twenty-six years, and all was well with my world. There is an old saying that "Sticks and stones may break my bones, but words will never hurt me." It is not just an old saying; it is an old lie.

Bob returned home from a business trip on a Sunday afternoon. He was sitting in his chair in our living room, and I was kneeling at his feet, expecting to have a "catch up" conversation, when with a few words of confession, my life shattered and my heart broke into a million little pieces. My husband was having an affair!

His words were hitting me, like the winds and the water slamming the foundation of my home. I knew I would not go under, but my husband must make a choice. His decision was to leave and take some time to think.

I went out to our deck to pray, and there the Lord made me a promise: "I will be your Son-light. I will walk with you through this, and when you get to the other side, you will have a good marriage." All I had to do was endure, breathe in and breathe out long enough, and Bob would come home. All would be well again.

I centered my life around that promise of restoration, and thirty years later, my dream came true; I had my "Happy Ending." Just as a few words had previously brought devastation, now a few words brought reconciliation and restoration.

Bob had married his mistress, but that marriage ended in divorce. He eventually moved to Mississippi, but Hurricane Katrina drove him back to Georgia. He began spending more time with us as a family, even going on our annual summer vacations. He invited all the guys on a cruise, at which time they became concerned about his health. I took him to the Veterans Administration hospital, and we did not get a good report. He wanted to play an even bigger part in our family, and go to church with us, so we made arrangements for his move into an assisted living facility just eight miles away.

We were enjoying this renewed family time, but one afternoon he called me to come because he was ill. As we were sitting at the supper table, he took my hand in his, and said, "I never stopped loving you. Please forgive me for all the hurt and pain I've caused you."

I replied, "Oh, Bob. I forgave you a long time ago. I love you, too."

We talked and laughed a lot during the short time left, agreeing that we were husband and wife—soulmates. His health was deteriorating rapidly and ten days later, he left me again. The Lord took him home; his work was finished, but mine was not.

I had received my miracle, but the "Happy Ending" was not as I had planned. I asked myself, "Is this all there is?"

I received an e-mail that stuck in my brain. I don't remember who sent it or who they were quoting, but it described "Guidance" as GOD, U and I DANCE. This was not scriptural, per se, but it made sense, as long as I let God lead!

I am not the first one to receive a vision or promise from God, experience what appears to be the death of the vision, then ultimately the fulfillment of the vision, and even beyond.

For instance, Mary was awestruck when the Angel Gabriel announced that she was "highly favored, the Lord is with you; blessed are you among women" (Luke 1:28, NKJV). He went on to say:

> And behold, you will conceive in your womb and bring forth a Son, and shall call His name JESUS. He will be great, and will be called the Son of the Highest, and the Lord God will give Him the throne of His father David. And He shall reign over the house of Jacob forever, and of His kingdom there shall be no end.
>
> —LUKE 1:31–33, NKJV

All Israel was anticipating the arrival of the Messiah; He would rule and reign, and set His people free. She was to be His mother! Probably the first warning that it would not be all sunshine, roses, and lollipops came from Simeon in the temple, when Mary and Joseph took Baby Jesus as their firstborn for dedication. He said:

> Behold, this Child is destined for the fall and rise of many in Israel, and for a sign which will

be spoken against. [Yes, a sword will pierce through your own soul also], that the hearts of many may be revealed.

—LUKE 2:34-35, NKJV

When Jesus started His ministry at the age of thirty, surely that would lead to His eventual inauguration as King. Instead, her beloved Son stirred up strife, and the Jewish religious leaders hated Him.

She must have been excited and so proud that day her Son was to speak in the synagogue at Nazareth, His hometown. But instead of being warmly received, the congregation was filled with wrath. Mary was shocked! They tried to throw Him off the cliff, but Jesus "passing through the midst of them, He went His way" (Luke 4:16–30, NKJV). At one point, she was so fearful for his safety that she and her other sons came to Jesus while He was preaching, "seeking" Him (Mark 3:31–35, NKJV), probably to take Him home, but Jesus would not be deterred.

Approximately two years later, Mary was huddled at the foot of the cross, weeping over her Son, Who had been bloodied and beaten, hardly recognizable as a man. What happened to the plan? But God was not finished. It was Friday, but Sunday was coming! It must have been John who told her the good news, for Jesus had entrusted her to his care (John 19:26–27, NKJV). Jesus was risen! What a reunion that had to be! Mary was present at His ascension, and also in the Upper Room when the Holy Spirit fell on the Day of Pentecost. Her Son was not just King of the Jews, but

He was King of kings and Lord of all creation. The day was coming when:

> Every knee shall bow to Me, and every tongue shall confess to God.
> —ROMANS 14:11, NKJV

God's plan for Mary and her Son went far beyond her wildest expectations! She is indeed "blessed among women" (Luke 1:28, NKJV).

God called Abram to leave his country to go to a land He would show him; God promised to make him a great nation, "and in you all the families of the earth shall be blessed" (Gen. 12:1–3, NKJV). Abram was seventy-five years of age at that time. Ten years passed but no children were born to Abram and his wife Sarai. Women are inclined to be a bit impatient, and Sarai decided to make things happen. Long story short, Abram and his wife's maid, Hagar, at the prompting of Sarai, had a son named Ishmael. Abram was eighty-six. We are still paying today for this bad decision.

When Abram was ninety-nine, the Lord appeared and entered into an everlasting covenant with him, declaring that he would be the father of many nations. At that time, God changed Abram's name to Abraham, and Sarai to Sarah. One year later, the son of promise was born, and they named him Isaac, meaning "laughter" because Sarah had said that God made her laugh (Gen. 21:6, NKJV).

Then God made an astonishing request of Abraham.

He was to offer his beloved son as a sacrifice (Gen. 22:2, NKJV). Abraham obeyed immediately, but we see his faith as he tells his servants to wait for them:

> Stay here with the donkey; the lad and I will go yonder and worship, and we will come back to you.
> —GENESIS 22:5, NKJV

Abraham intended to return with his son. And he did! At the moment Abraham raised the knife to slay his son in obedience to God's command, God intervened, and He said:

> Do not lay your hand on the lad, or do anything to him; for now I know that you fear God, since you have not withheld your son, your only son, from Me.
> —GENESIS 22:12, NKJV

Isaac is a type of the Lord Jesus Christ, God's only begotten Son. Like Jesus, Isaac was obedient to his father and willing to become the sacrifice.

Abraham's beloved wife Sarah died at the age of 127 years. When "Abraham was old, well advanced in age" (Gen. 24:1), he dispatched his oldest servant, to find a wife for Isaac, and we read of the success of his mission in Genesis 24. Verse 67 is poignant. "Then Isaac brought her into his mother's tent; and he took Rebekah and she became his wife, and he loved her."

Rebekah bears twins, Esau and Jacob; God refers to them as "two nations" (Gen. 25:23, NKJV), the Arabs and the Jews. From Jacob the twelve tribes come, the foundation of the Jewish nation, and God's covenant promises begin to quickly unfold.

But that is not the end the story for Abraham. He "again took a wife, and her name was Keturah" (Gen. 25:1, NKJV); she bore six more children! Abraham died at the ripe old age of 175, and, after making provisions for the other members of his family, he "gave all that he had to Isaac" (Gen. 25:5). Indeed, Isaac was the Son of Promise; however, God took Abraham exceedingly beyond his original happy ending.

Consider Joseph, who had two dreams of being in a position of high authority. He was Daddy Jacob's "favorite," plus being a "dreamer," and his brothers were not impressed. On one occasion Jacob sent Joseph to look for the other sons, and they seized this opportunity to sell him to some passing Midianites, who in turn sold him to Potiphar, an officer of Pharaoh's army in Egypt (Gen. 37). Joseph was a teenager, seventeen years old. Potiphar's wife took a shine to Joseph, but he resisted her advances. This made her very angry and she had him thrown into prison. Even in prison, Joseph was granted God's favor (Gen. 39:21). There he interpreted the dreams of the Pharaoh's butler and baker, and he requested that they remember him (Gen. 40:14, NKJV).

Two full years passed, when the Pharaoh had a dream that no one could interpret. Then the butler remembered Joseph, who came and gave the interpretation. There would be seven years of plenty, followed by seven years of famine. Joseph proposed a plan, Pharaoh agreed, and Joseph was appointed as ruler in Egypt, second only to the Pharaoh (Gen. 41).

God works in mysterious ways, and because of famine in Israel, the sons were sent to Egypt to buy food. The plot thickened, and the end result was that Joseph's brothers and even Jacob, his father, bowed down to him, fulfilling Joseph's original dreams.

God used Joseph to save not only his family, but the Jewish and Egyptian nations. Joseph continued to officiate, preserve, and protect all the people God put in his charge. He went exceedingly and abundantly beyond his dreams.

> Dreams do come true; we have God's Word on it: Don't be impatient for the Lord to act! Keep traveling steadily along His pathway and in due season He will honor you with every blessing... For the good man—the blameless, the upright, the man of peace—he has a wonderful future ahead of him. For him there is a happy ending.
> —Psalm 37:34, 37 TLB

The fulfillment of dreams and promises kept does not signal that the dance is over. The music plays on and we dance until our Father says it's time to go home. Sometimes we even dance in the rain, but that's OK. We're going beyond!

Chapter One

Three Generations on Mission in Mexico

THIS WAS MY fifth mission to Reynosa, Mexico, and I was particularly excited. I had been on seventeen short-term missions to twelve various countries, but this was the first time any member of my family had accompanied me. My daughter Stacey, her husband Russell, and their two daughters, Abby, age seventeen, and Maddie, age fifteen, were probably even more thrilled because it was their first foreign mission. As an added blessing, we brought Jessica, age seventeen, whom I had known since the day she was born; she was family. We were going on their spring break, April 2009.

This trip, as well as the other four to Reynosa, was led by my dear friend David, founder of Looking Unto

Jesus Ministries, and our destination was Maranatha Iglesia de Dios, a church pastored by the Reverends Daniel and Adamina. We were to speak at services held in the church, and minister at the altar as the congregation responded. In Reynosa you could count on a good response. The faith of the people is always great; therefore, there are many healing miracles, but the greatest miracle is conversion—when Jesus comes into a heart. The plan included having our meals, excluding breakfast, in the homes of various church members. They invite their unchurched neighbors, and at the conclusion of the meal, we minister to the needs of those present. Each trip is unique, and while I shared my former experiences with my family by way of preparation, you just cannot tell what the Lord has in store. This one turned out to be a "doozy!"

We met David and another team member, Lester, at the departure gate. Two other members of the team and Warren were driving a van down that had been donated to the Reynosa church. As we were about to board the plane in Atlanta, Russell discovered to his dismay that his carry-on bag, which included his clothes and Bible, had been left at the curb when Stacey checked in their one large suitcase. There was no time for a search. Stacey was also upset because her Bible and sermon notes were also in that bag. She said when she put the notes in her Bible the preceding evening she had a dreadful feeling that she would never see them again.

Here was our first test, actually second test, because

Russell could not find a parking place at the airport and since time was fleeting, he took a chance and created a space. You could say, he took a "park faith." Thus, he had a lot on his mind. What was he going to wear in Mexico, and would the van be there when we returned to Atlanta?

On the first leg of the journey, from Atlanta to Houston, I sat next to Joann, who was going to meet her sisters. One of the sisters, Alice, had been diagnosed with breast cancer, and they were to accompany her to her doctor's appointment the following Monday. They were a support team. Joann was a Christian, and she readily accepted my offer to pray with her for her sister's healing.

There were no opportunities to share on the last leg of the trip from Houston to McAllen, Texas. Pastor Adamina met us, and we had prayer time right there on the grassy area next to the entrance. Adamina is dynamic, to put it mildly, and she has "church" anywhere, anytime, anyplace. When we explained Russell's dilemma, she took us to the mall across the street so he could get underwear and socks. Then she reported that a man in North Georgia had sent clothes to them the day before, and they were all large sizes. Russell is 6'4", which is much larger than the average Mexican man. When we got to the church, he was able to get more than enough to cover our time there. Some of the pants were a tad short, but of no consequence. The ladies who managed the clothing at the church were delighted to be able to bless Russell. Most of the time, the team is bringing items to them, and this was their opportunity to minister to our needs. God showed that He was way ahead of us, and He provided bountifully.

The girls were shocked when Adamina announced they would be called at the first service that evening. Stacey already knew in her heart that she would preach, so had prepared on the plane, rewriting her notes from memory and borrowing a Bible. I was so pleased when all three girls did a skit together, and each one shared scripture that was meaningful to her. Abby and Maddie ended with a duet, "You Are the Treasure That I Seek." Stacey's sermon covered three points: The Word, prayer, and the Holy Spirit. I could not have been more proud of my young ladies.

Many came forward to the altar for prayer so the entire team was busy. How I wish we would see that in our home churches. Our Mexican brothers and sisters expect God to move, and He does!

On my fourth mission to Reynosa in December 2007, I had occasion to pray with Peter, a handsome teenager who had leukemia. The team had received good reports since then, and I was looking forward to seeing him again on this trip; however, this was not to be, as Peter had died in the fall of 2008. He had done well for almost a year, but then the Lord called him home. I talked with his brother and sister that evening and later met his father and mother. They were all still grieving, but Adamina had a dream about Peter, in which he was dressed in cowboy clothes, his favorite attire, and he was healed and very happy. This dream comforted the family

We ended our long, fruitful first day with a supper of tamales and beans at the parsonage. Authentic Mexican food is "delicioso!"

We began our first full day, Sunday, with a traditional Mexican breakfast, which means refried beans and tortillas are always included, along with eggs and guacamole. My girls were obedient to do all that was asked of them, full of grace and beauty, eager to help. I was proud as a peacock!

We had devotions and communion in the living room, with Pastor Danny joining us. He is a talented singer, guitarist, preacher, and has a daily radio show, yet he is quiet and reserved. When he does speak, it is profound, and I am expectant when he is able to be with us. Adamina is more vocal and exuberant. When she is present, you know things are going to happen; it is in the atmosphere. They are a dynamic duo!

We went to the market, where the locals have their different shops. One of the shopkeepers allows Adamina to preach in front of her store, and as Adamina was presenting the Gospel, our team gave out tracts and conversed as best we could with the people. At the conclusion, five accepted Jesus as their Lord and Savior. We topped off our morning with some shopping, which is a marvelous way to build good relations, and, of course, you cannot come to the market and not partake of their yummy ice cream.

Next stop was lunch at Mannie's home, with his

wife, son Saul and daughter Deena. After a nice meal, we ministered to their neighbor, Margaret, whose daughter was treating her shamefully. She agreed that she must forgive her daughter, and we promised we would pray as well for her to be saved. Then Margaret herself invited Jesus into her heart, and she was filled with the Holy Spirit.

Another guest, Ruby, who was six months pregnant, also had a forgiveness issue. When she did forgive, she was gloriously saved and received the baptism of the Holy Spirit. We prayed for the unborn baby, her pregnancy, and a delivery with no trauma.

The host couple had a previous home, which was infested with worms, and now had the same problem in this house, so Adamina broke the curse. David and Lester prayed for their daughter Deena for healing of her back and legs.

This was Palm Sunday and the evening service was extra-special. The children entered the back of the sanctuary and proceeded to the front, dressed in ancient Jewish costumes and waving palm branches. The music was joyful. (Stacey calls it "Mexico loud.") Russell gave his testimony, sharing how he had been a former wild man, thought he was in love, but the girl ditched him and broke his heart; however, this led him to Christ. Now he has a beautiful wife (my daughter Stacey) and two darling daughters! This was special to me, because he is my "son-in-love."

David shared a testimony on forgiveness, and Lester preached. When he gave the invitation, the altar was full. Many forgave offenses, and then were filled with the Spirit. I prayed with a man and his wife. He had just lost his job; and they wanted more of the Holy Spirit. Their son was with them, weeping over his father's plight. All three were filled with the *Shekinah* ("weighty") glory of God and were unable to stand. Christians call this being "slain in the Spirit." As the young man lay on the floor, he began laughing with joy.

I prayed with two elderly ladies for healing; one had arthritis and the other had stomach pains. After I finished ministering, I looked over to my side and saw David praying for my girls. They, too, were "slain in the Spirit."

The church ministry was over, but there was more to be done before our day ended. Supper was at the home of Ivy and Allen. Their small son, who loved our girls, was there, as well as Ivy's parents, Freda and Mark. Freda was having eye problems, so I prayed for her healing, and the Holy Spirit poured into her. Her husband wanted strength and he was touched. David prayed for the hosts and their son. It was a sweet ending to a full day.

It was Monday, and Adamina, David, and Warren had to get the van registered in Mexico around 7:00 a.m. The rest of the team prepared breakfast, and afterward, we had devotions in the living room, each one sharing what had been most meaningful to him or her thus far. My girls loved being in the homes, the music and ministry, while Russell loved the humility of the people. Then we toured the church, where they were now working on the third floor. On my first trip in 1998, they were just beginning construction, paying as they built.

Lunch was at Maria's home, a repeat visit for me. Her specialty is inviting unsaved neighbors to her home when the missionaries come. She is an excellent cook, and it was here that I learned to say "delici-o-so" and "de nada," which means "*it is nothing*," their reply when I would thank them for something. It was our joke. True to form, two of the guests accepted Christ and were filled with the Spirit. The Holy Spirit fell on pretty Natividad. Stacey prayed for our hostess, Maria, and she fell out under the Spirit. David called on Abby to pray for Louise to be filled with the Spirit, and she also was unable to stand. Stacey wept as she watched her daughter ministering.

Some of the team went to the city to get the van, and then to the airport to collect Gary and Hank of Life Line Ministry, who had come to install tile flooring in the parsonage. Meanwhile, Stacey, Maddie, Jessica, and I walked through the neighborhood, taking pictures of the kids, who are real "hams."

Pastor Danny had taken David, Lester, and Russell to the radio station for his broadcast, but there were problems and he was unable to air. I regretted this, especially for Russell.

At the evening service, the children of the church did a skit about Jesus chasing the money changers out of the temple. Delightful! Warren gave his testimony and I preached. Again the altar was full and there was much ministry. It was thrilling to see my entire family praying for others. My cup runneth over!

Supper was at Paul's house: beef soft tacos, bean soup, and ice cream. Afterwards, we ministered to the family. They already knew Jesus and were Spirit-filled, so it was a time of blessing. Thank You, Jesus!

Suddenly, it was Tuesday, our last full day of ministry. After a hearty breakfast with our additional guests from Life Line, it was back to Reynosa to get license plates, but there was an error in the paperwork, so it would be "mañana" (tomorrow), which is so typical in Mexico. We were able to purchase the tile flooring, which made Adamina very happy.

After another stop at a local market for the refreshments we needed, we arrived at the Juvenile Detention Center, one of my favorite places for ministry. It saddened me to see these young people in jail, but it was a marvelous opportunity to show them the love of Christ. On all my visits in previous years, there had been numerous salvations, and Adamina had continued to disciple these young converts. I wanted my grandchildren to have the experience of seeing how precious our freedom is, how God can change hearts and give hope in desperate circumstances. We had fifteen young male inmates, and Russell was a bit uneasy. Our three girls gave touching testimonies, and then Russell emphasized that he was "watching" over them, pounding his fist into his hand. The boys laughed because they knew what he meant; however, Russell's little talk also pierced hearts. Then some of the more seasoned shared, testifying of the Lord's faithfulness for the long haul. We were all excited when two accepted Christ as their Savior—Gustav and Jesus, who was extra blessed because of his name. The rest already had a relationship with the Lord. Then it was party time. The boys were tickled to have these pretty girls serving them, and there was laughter all around. It was sad to leave them behind these bars, but there was the promise of a future and a hope, and we knew God had good plans for them (Jer. 29:11).

We proceeded to the James home, located a few blocks from the church. I had been there on other missions, and it was good to see old friends. The meal, as usual, was outstanding: chicken and vegetable soup, plus cantaloupe and watermelon that was so refreshing. We ministered to the family, and there were lots of them, from wee little ones up to our elderly host and hostess. But there was a special one the Lord brought to us that day, youth pastor Ronald's former wife, Louise. They had gone through a nasty divorce, and she lived with another man for about eighteen months, leaving him to return to the James home. Meanwhile, Ronald had come to Christ and was filled with the Holy Spirit. He wanted his wife back and their marriage restored; however, there was a trust issue and he was not helping her financially. Pastor Adamina had been counseling both of them, and I was able to share my testimony with the wife, stressing that forgiveness was not an option for her, but a commandment. God wanted her to be free, and for her to release her husband so he could also be free. She saw this truth and from her heart forgave Ronald, at which time the Lord embraced her and she was filled with the Holy Spirit! There was victory in the house! Sad to say, I received a later report that the relationship remains broken, but there is always hope.

At the evening service, the entire team came forward and shared what the mission had meant to them. My Stacey was weeping; she called it "Mom tears of joy." Russell and our three girls had been blessed beyond measure. I was bursting with pride, coupled with humility that God had chosen us for this special time, and laughter coupled with sadness that my Bob was not here to share this unforgettable occasion.

Judy gave a heart-rending testimony of deliverance from abuse, drugs, and the Mafia, and everyone was moved to tears. She is an awesome woman of God, and it is always a joy to serve with her. Our new friend Hank preached a powerful message, very high volume, and the people loved it. It was amazing that he was stressing the same points Stacey had in her sermon that first night: prayer, the Word, and the power of the Holy Spirit in our lives. We had come full circle!

At the altar call, it seemed the entire church came forward. The Spirit was moving at the invitation of the people, and they were not able to stand in the Shekinah glory. As I was praying for others, I glanced over to see my three girls lying on the floor in front of the altar. They would never be the same.

As I was praying for Vernon, who was so worried

about his father getting a job, I received a word of encouragement for him. The Lord was very pleased because of his love, concern, and honor for his parents, and wanted him to rest assured that his heavenly Father was in control, and all was and would be well.

One mother wanted prayer for the safety of her son who had gone to the U.S. to get work. He was sending money home to support the family, but she felt the price was too high; he might never come back to her. He could be killed!

Violence also concerned another mother, whose son was a mechanic and worked in a garage. The owner was paying a gang in exchange for their "protection." Her son had been beaten several times, but he could find no other work, and felt trapped in his situation.

When our ministry ended, we went to our last supper at the beautiful home of Tammy, who was the girlfriend of Edward, Adamina's eldest son. This celebration included not only our team and our two new mission friends, but the entire gang of musicians and special family members of Danny and Adamina—that radical, Spirit-filled bunch that was so dear to our hearts. It was party time, and we know how our Jesus loves celebrations!

It was morning before we knew it, and time to go home. How did that happen? We had just arrived! We tried to leave early, but that never happens in Mexico. There seems to be an unwritten law, and it involves being late. There was a long, long, long line at the border crossing, and dear Russell faced the dilemma of no bathroom facilities; however, good missionaries know how to improvise and fortunately, I had an empty water bottle. Ronald was driving and trying his best not to laugh at his gringo friend. I will say that Russell's presence made the trip a lot more exciting, as he brought life, laughter, and joy to all.

We made our plane by a matter of minutes, so it was a very hasty goodbye to our friends. The flight from McAllen to Houston was very short, and I sat by Maddie. I could catch my breath since Maddie knew Jesus very well! From Houston to Atlanta, I was seated by a charismatic Christian lady, so she witnessed to me! In Houston our gate number was changed, so it was another mad dash to the new gate, where they were holding the plane for us. I had no seat partner for the last leg of the journey, and it was nice just to be quiet and reflect on our adventure.

Abby told me once that when she is in a group and she speaks about me as her grandmother, she always says that I smuggled Bibles into China and talked a policeman out of a ticket. I hoped that now she would add that she served as a missionary to Mexico with her G'ma Bet.

Upon arrival in Atlanta, Russell checked with Continental Air Lines to see if they had his bag, to no avail. Abby checked with Delta, since Delta tags were on the suitcase, but they also said "no." We were delighted to discover the van had not been towed, so we were not striking out totally. We celebrated with a steak dinner because we had missed lunch, and because it was just good to be home! When we walked in the door at home, there were three telephone messages from Delta, urging the Woods to claim their suitcase! As we were about God's business, He was about ours.

Several years prior to this trip, a Christian brother had prophesied to me that not only would my husband return, but also my daughter and her husband would serve on foreign missions; therefore, I was not surprised to have them with me in Reynosa. I thought they would go when the girls were away at college or "out of the nest." To have both girls, plus our sweet Jessica, went beyond my expectations!

Chapter Two

Podiums, Places, and People

WHEN MY FIRST book, *Around the World in Seventy Years*, was published, the Lord promised to give me "podiums, places and people," because He had "a plan and a purpose." His people were fainting along the way and I was to encourage them. I thought when you wrote a book, you just sat back and collected the royalties. The publisher did all the marketing; only the famous went on promotion tours. God had a different plan for me. I knew that *Nothing Wasted*, my second book, was included in this plan, giving me a double-barreled message.

God has truly kept His word as I have spoken to small groups mostly, and occasionally to entire congregations in the major Protestant denominations. I have spoken to elementary and high school students, as well as senior citizens; there have been women circles, mission groups, and book clubs. I have led women's retreats, and have even been invited to teach on topics other than the two books I have written. The doors to Women's Aglow, AARP, Rotary, and Kiwanis have opened as well. Wow! Who would have thought it!

On one occasion I was invited to participate in a book signing at a mega charismatic church. There would be two authors at the first service and two at the second. I was so excited that the Lord would give me this boost, as I had a garage full of books, but a few days prior to the proposed event, I received a call from the secretary of the assistant pastor in charge, at which time I was politely "uninvited" because I was not a member of their church. I had given my church affiliation up front, and apparently that was overlooked. I was very disappointed and had a little talk with the Lord. He simply asked me a question: "Who gets the glory at a book signing?" I replied, "The author does." End of conversation.

I have to suppress my laughter every time I stand to speak. It is like a little joke between the Holy Spirit and me. I have shared this incident before, but as I was recalling it recently, I saw a new truth I had over-looked in earlier years. I remember so vividly as a teenager standing on an auditorium stage at Hapeville High School, trying out for cheerleader. The procedure was to compose an original cheer, teach it to the students, as you did the accompanying motions. Five would be chosen that day out of a field of about ten.

Donna, who preceded me, was very popular, and the students were wildly applauding, when the teacher in charge told me to go on the stage. I declined, as there was so much noise and Donna was soaking it in. I was literally pushed on stage as Donna exited. The students continued to yell and I just stood there. Finally I said, "You can shut up now!" They yelled even louder, and then they were laughing at me. It seemed there were millions of faces staring at me, like little postage stamps, but two stood out from the rest. My former boyfriend had moved back from Florida, and he was sitting with his new girlfriend. As I began to speak, my voice cracked with fear, not the best qualification for a cheerleader. I did teach them my cheer, going through all the motions, and gladly exited the stage post haste. It came as no surprise to me when the announcement was made the following day that I had not been chosen. There was a special assembly and the five new cheerleaders led the students in my cheer! They wanted my work, but they did not want me. I can still see all those faces today and hear my cracking voice.

What I see now is that I was destined to be a cheerleader for Christ. He will never reject me. When I speak now, I know I am there only because I have been chosen "for such a time as this" (Esther 4:14, NKJV), and "I can do all things through Christ who strengthens me" (Phil. 4:13, NKJV). There are no small things in His kingdom!

I believe that the miracle of all miracles here on earth occurs when a fellow human being recognizes the reality of Christ and accepts Him as Lord and Savior; therefore, I was ecstatic when my friend Jay, from a town in South Georgia, called to tell me he had given my book *Around the World* to a friend visiting from London, England. After reading the book, she asked him to answer some questions. As he did, she came to know Christ personally!

A book club had been studying *Nothing Wasted*, and I was invited to share a presentation and conclude with a question and answer session, which can be a scary thing. One young woman was waving her hand furiously, so I went to her first. She said she was mad at me! That was a bit shocking, so I asked why. She said I should have married the man who held my hand; that I could have prayed for Bob from a distance; that he was not worth waiting for as he was just a woman chaser! She felt I deserved better. That was a rather kind sentiment on her part toward me, but she missed the point. I was following the directions of my Lord, and my Bob was loved into the kingdom. I did get my happy ending!

After speaking to a reunion group comprised of both men and women, using examples from both books, a woman and her son wanted to talk. She was probably in her mid-forties and he was in his twenties. Her husband had left several years ago, and she was very bitter. She said that she did not know why, but as I spoke she could not stop crying, and she still could not stop. What was happening? I replied that the Lord wanted her to be free, and to do that they must forgive.

Forgiveness is not an option with a Christian. Jesus forgave from the Cross, and He has instructed us to forgive so that we can be forgiven in that same manner (Matt. 6:12). She did not think she was able to forgive, but she was willing to be made willing, and I led her in prayer. The Lord wanted to heal her wounded spirit, and also her son. This was a divine appointment!

At the conclusion of my talk at a Methodist Women's Circle, the President introduced me to Marjorie, the custodian of the church. Marjorie said the Lord told her that morning to go on to the church, but she was protesting. She told the Lord that she would not be able to do any work because of the meeting, but He insisted she go anyway. She said she was cleaning in the restroom adjacent to the fellowship hall, and she could hear every word I said through the vent. She had been praying for her wayward son for a very long time and was discouraged. I took Marjorie by the hand, and we went to a private corner to pray with great confidence because the Lord had brought her there at that particular time. Most assuredly, He would answer our prayer of agreement for her prodigal son!

At that same meeting, the president of the circle was facing surgery the next day. She did not want to make a fuss, but I explained that she was robbing her sisters because when she came through with a glowing report, their faith would be strengthened. She agreed, so I anointed her with oil and prayed the prayer of faith (James 5:14–15). Her sisters-in-Christ laid hands on her and prayed along with me. She did indeed get a good report following the surgery, and the announcement was made at the Wednesday night service to a rejoicing congregation. Here was another example of "Nothing Wasted."

I received an e-mail from a woman in Malaysia, the subject being "Reflections on Nothing Wasted." Yi Len had been married twenty years when her husband left her and their six-year-old daughter for another woman. Her spirit was wounded and her heart was broken. She wanted me to know that there was a woman on the other side of the world who was hurting, and my book had helped her. We have continued to stay in touch. This past Christmas she wrote me a glowing testimony of how much she had grown in her faith, and how she had given her testimony in two churches. I replied that she had actually witnessed in more than two, as I have been sharing her testimony on numerous occasions. She has come forth like shining gold!

My contact person at a local Methodist church e-mailed me to say they were very excited that the author of these two books was coming in person to speak to them. It seemed that my appearance would validate what I had written. That made me very happy also, and then I had a light bulb moment! Jesus is the Author of the best-selling book of all time, the Holy Bible, and He is coming back in person for His Bride, the Church. His Word will indeed be validated, made alive! Even so, "Come quickly, Lord Jesus!"

The Lord leads me to His chosen "podiums, places, and people" in very unique and clever ways. Two friends of mine belonged to a District Missionary Society, which opened the door for me to speak at one of their meetings, my subject being Zimbabwe. At the luncheon afterwards, a lady wanted to purchase both books but she did not have the money or her checkbook with her. I gave her the books and said she could mail me a check later, which she did. She included a thank-you note, saying she started *Nothing Wasted* the very next day and could not put it down. (Authors love to hear that!) She gave me the name of her church and her pastor's name. I sent him a packet with both books. Shortly thereafter, he sent a letter asking if I would be the speaker at their fifth annual Racial Reconciliation Day. I affirmed immediately that I would be honored.

I arrived early on that special Sunday, so the pastor and I could meet and pray. In our conversation, he told me that I was not their first choice, but he had invited the president of their association, and this person had belatedly replied he would not be coming without any reason given. The pastor said he simply did nothing to obtain a new speaker; then he got my books and decided to call me. (I was "second choice.") I remembered hearing a general of the Salvation Army share that he had done a lot of things for the Lord that he was not the best qualified to do, simply because the better qualified candidate said "no" but he said "yes!" I told the pastor that anytime the better qualified dropped out, he could call on me.

The service was amazing, if I do say so myself. They said it was the first time a woman had spoken in their pulpit, and I thought they meant for Reconciliation Day, but another pastor friend said that was true for that denomination. This was indeed an honor! As I spoke, the people laughed (at the appropriate places) and some dabbed the tears from their eyes. They were so warm, friendly, and responsive, and when I finished, they stood and clapped for me! I was so happy that I had been used to bless them.

But there was more, because we had Holy Communion, served by the men of the church. After they served the elements, they came to the front and stood tall, like the disciples of Jesus. Then the lights were dimmed, and in deepest reverence, we partook of the bread and the wine. My heart was overflowing.

But there was more, because it was Racial Reconciliation Day. Two teenagers, a girl and boy, gave testimonies honoring Dr. Martin Luther King, Jr. The worship leader, who "happened" to be the lady from the Missionary Society, had us all cross our arms, hold hands, and sing together, "We Shall Overcome." I felt such a bond, a kinship, with my new brothers and sisters. I understood them better. How could I contain any more joy?

But there was more, as the pastor and I stood at the exit to greet the congregation as they left, I was shaking hands and hugging necks, meeting my new family of God. A little boy asked me if the books were just for grown-ups. I said, "Would you like to go on missions?" and he replied "Yes." I gave him *Around the World* and said it was just for him.

But there was more. We had been stuffed spiritually, and now we had a feast of soul-food laid out for us: fried chicken, biscuits, cornbread, turnip greens, sweet potatoes, macaroni and cheese, chocolate cake, coconut cake, and iced tea! I sat with the pastor and his lovely wife, and some new friends. The conversation was sparkling, lively, encouraging and spiced with laughter.

But there was more. The pastor had been suffering from a throat condition for many months, and as he and his wife walked me back to the sanctuary to retrieve my books, I asked if we could pray for him. His wife stood on one side and I stood on the other, as we prayed for his healing. A pastor definitely needs his voice; it is an important instrument. Our Lord could surely see the logic in that, and so we stand on His promise:

> Now this is the confidence that we have in Him, that if we ask anything according to His will, He hears us. And if we know that He hears us, whatever we ask, we know that we have the petitions that we have asked of Him.
> —1 JOHN 5:14–15, NKJV

His wife reported to me that her husband said he felt much better since we prayed!

It was my heart's desire to be God's instrument that day, to bring glory to Him, and to bless His church. But you just cannot out give God, for I received the greater blessing!

Another example of that is a double-header I had

in Hapeville, Georgia. I grew up in Hapeville, and so did my husband. We moved there when I was five, I attended elementary and high school, and accepted Christ in the Presbyterian Church, where Bob and I married. Bob's family was very active in the Methodist Church, where his grandmother played the organ, Daddy sang in the choir, and Uncle Wayne and Aunt Libby attended Sunday school. Uncle Maurice was the postmaster and Aunt Bernice was principal at College Street Elementary. Some folks thought my Dad was "Meatball" Terry, but I assured them my Dad was no "Meatball." He was a U.S. Marine in World War II, serving in Iwo Jima on that infamous flag-raising day. My Mom was an awesome stay-at-home mother who thought I could do anything!

Bob and I attempted to run a dry cleaning business on Central Avenue, and thankfully, he was good at poker because we used his winnings to buy groceries, as our business slowly drained us of all our assets. We called it our "Laughing Place." Hapeville is my home town.

I had taken my books to both churches, the Methodist and the Baptist. They are located on opposite sides of the street. I spoke at the Baptist Church on Tuesday morning to their "Young at Hearts," and to the "Wonderful Wednesday" Methodists on, of course, Wednesday. Both meetings were lots of fun, like family reunions. A friend of mine uses the phrase, "The Lord showed up and showed out," and He truly did just that.

At the conclusion of my talk at the Baptist Church, the director of the Hapeville Historical Society advised that my books were being placed in the city's museum located in the old depot!

A friend once commented that I must be elated that my books are in the Library of Congress. Of course, I am; however, I consider being in the City of Hapeville's museum in the old depot an honor that goes far beyond. I could not be happier!

Chapter Three

Because God Said So!

THE LORD OPENED another door for me as a part of my "beyond" process. This one took me way "beyond" my comfort zone. I believe He delights in seeing us stretch and grow, just as parents delight in seeing the progress of their children as new vistas open in their lives. For example, my granddaughter Maddie is an excellent runner—everyone knows it; she even looks like a runner—tall and lean. But Maddie discovered a talent she didn't know she had. Maddie is a dynamite swimmer. What a delight to see her develop that surprise gift!

I received a call from my dear friend Walt concerning the United Methodist Men's annual retreat to be held in April 2010 at Jefferson United Methodist Church in Jefferson, Georgia. He was asking me to serve as a co-speaker with my dear friend, Pastor James. James is dynamic; he has a powerful testimony of being a former member of the Mafia and being saved in prison. Now he is an ordained Methodist preacher.

"You're asking me?"

This was mind-blowing. However, the Word says that our Lord does delight in choosing "the foolish things of the world to confound the wise; and God has chosen the weak things of the world to confound the things which are mighty" (1 Cor. 1:27, NKJV). That way He gets all the glory!

I didn't just fall off the turnip truck, so I gladly accepted the invitation. My Lord had never failed me, and I saw this as another door of opportunity. He had promised "podiums, places, and people."

We were asked for our thoughts on a theme for the retreat, and the phrase that kept coming to my mind was "Because God Said So!" In my youth, my parents would give me orders, and I would rebel, asking "Why?" The answer was, "Because I said so; that's why!" That was the end of the matter.

We need to take God's Word today as the end of the matter. There was a popular saying for years: "God said so, I believe it, and that settles it." Whether we believe it or not, "God said so; that settles it!"

We also wanted to emphasize Jesus as being the Rock that does not roll, our solid foundation, and we wanted everyone to come, not just the Methodist men, but women, singles, and couples. Therefore, the broad invitation was to "Come to the Rock—Because God Says So!"

This was an all day event, with James opening, me following him (Lord, have mercy), then the men and women separating into sessions after lunch. James was with the men, of course, and I was with the women. (Wonder how that would shake things up if we ever switched?) When we returned to the main session, I spoke, and then James closed with an altar call. We tend to overuse the word "special," but it really was special. Thank You, Lord!

And now, dear reader, I want to share with you the messages I delivered on that red letter day in my life. Just imagine yourself in the sanctuary in the Rock Church at Jefferson. There are stained glass windows that catch the sun, reminding you of the grand cathedrals in Europe. The walls are a dark wood, reaching high to the ceiling, like Noah's ark, and the carpet is rich red. I think it is one of God's favorite places. Come with me as we go "beyond."

Chapter Four

You Can be Faith-Full in a Faith-Less World:
Building Your Faith God's Way

THIS IS THE first session and I am very nervous. This is not a bad thing, because if I were confident, I would not be leaning on the Holy Spirit. The Bible says that when we are weak, we are dynamite (2 Cor. 12:10). I have my visuals: my Friendship Bread starter in a plastic bag, along with the recipe. I didn't realize the starter would be so pungent, but it is what it is, and I must "glow with the flow." I start with my gratitude for the invitation, which is always a good place to start.

The Message

I've got some bad news and I've got some good news! Which do you want first? (Their response is mixed.)

The bad news is that everything in our world that can be shaken will be shaken.

The good news is that we have received a kingdom that cannot be shaken (Hag. 2:6–7; Heb. 12:28).

It doesn't take a rocket scientist to see that we are living today in a shaking world. Would you have ever thought that our government would be in the car business and in the banking business, or that we would have same sex marriages, prayer would be ruled unconstitutional, and the things we read about in Sodom and Gomorrah would be acceptable and even celebrated in our very own nation?

We got trouble, folks, "right here in River City—Trouble with a great big capital 'T.'" But why are we surprised? Jesus said we would have "T"—tribulation, but to cheer up, for He has overcome the world (John 16:33).

When we are in Christ, and He is in us, we also are overcomers. We overcome by the blood of the Lamb (what Jesus accomplished for us through His crucifixion and resurrection), and by the word of our testimony (Rev. 12:11). Testimony is a statement under oath, a declaration of what you believe is the truth; it is evidence. Boiled down, it is your faith.

Faith is the anchor of our soul. Faith will hold us steady in the midst of the storm.

When my husband announced to me that he was leaving after twenty-six years of marriage, his words came at me like the winds, the waves, and the waters. I was being hit from every side, but I had that knowing in my soul; I was not going under. My house was on the Rock, not on shifting sand. Your "knower knows," in spite of the circumstances.

A gospel singer shared his experience of going through a hurricane. He was living on a houseboat tied to the dock in a fishing village. The storm raged all night, tossing his boat up and down, slamming it against the dock. At last the hurricane moved on, and it was calm again. In the morning he went for breakfast at the local restaurant, and he said to the folks gathered there, "If I had known I was coming through it, I would have enjoyed it more!"

Oh, to have that "resting" faith in the midst of the storm.

In the Greek (this always sounds impressive), faith is defined in *Vine's Expository Dictionary of New Testament Words* as "a firm persuasion, a conviction based upon hearing; is used in the New Testament always of faith in God or Christ, or things spiritual... trust...trustworthiness."[1]

Webster's New American Dictionary says that it is "complete trust or confidence, to believe, accept as true, unquestioning, especially religious belief, loyalty."

The Bible says: "*Now* faith is the substance of things hoped for, the evidence of things not seen" (Heb. 11:1, NKJV, emphasis added).

Now faith is. If it's not *now*, it's not faith. If you push it off into the future, then it is hope, not faith. Hope is like the blueprint; faith is the substance, the building.

Jesus said, "Whatever things you ask, *when you pray, believe* that you receive them, and you will have them" (Mark 11:24, NKJV, emphasis added). So the time to believe, to have faith, is when you pray.

It's the Abraham faith. Abraham was fully persuaded that what God had promised, He was able to perform (Rom. 4:21). Our faith is in a God who is able. He is All Powerful and All Mighty; He is a God of integrity. We can believe *because God said so!*

When I was a kid, questioning my dad with "Why do I have to do this," or "Why this," or "Why that," he would put an end to my "Whys" with "Because I said so!" That was the end of the matter. So it is with our heavenly Father; His Word is the end of the matter.

The Thomas faith says, "I'll believe it when I see it." If you have it, you don't need faith. In God's kingdom we believe whether we see it or not, "for we walk by faith, not by sight" (2 Cor. 5:7). The world says, "Seeing is believing," but God says, "Believing is seeing."

Listen to this translation:

> The fundamental fact of existence is that this trust in God, this faith, is the firm foundation under everything that makes life worth living. It's our handle on what we can't see. The act of faith is what distinguished our ancestors, set them above the crowd. By faith, we see the

world called into existence by God's word, what
we see created by what we don't see.
—HEBREWS, 11:1–3, THE MESSAGE

The Bible says that Jesus *spoke* the worlds into existence; God created something out of nothing (Heb.
11:3).

Satan challenged God to a contest. He said he could
do everything God could do. God accepted the challenge. Satan bent down to scoop some dirt to make an
earth. God said, "Get your own dirt!"

There is an account in Mark 11, starting with verse
12, where Jesus is hungry and he goes to this fig tree,
but finds no figs. He curses the tree, saying it would
never bear fruit again. The next day, Jesus and the disciples return the same way, and the disciples are amazed
to see that the tree had withered away. They ask, "How
did you do that?"

Jesus replies, "Have faith in God."

But we will never believe God until we believe that
He is believable; that He is faithful.

In Exodus 34:6–7, the Lord God described Himself
as "merciful and gracious, longsuffering, and abounding
in goodness and truth, keeping mercy for thousands,
forgiving iniquity and transgression and sin" (NKJV).

It's not bragging when it's the truth! This is a God
who is trustworthy. And, of course, God is love, and
God is good—all the time!

In Hebrews, chapter 11 (The Hall of Faith), verse 6:
"But without faith, *it is* impossible to please *Him,* for he

who comes to God must believe that He is, and *that* He is a rewarder of them that diligently seek Him" (NKJV).

Hudson Taylor, the great missionary to China, was going through a faith crisis. He wrote: "I strove for faith, but it would not come. I tried to exercise it, but in vain...When my agony of soul was at its height, a sentence in a letter from dear McCarthy was used to remove the scales from my eyes, and the Spirit of God revealed to me the truth of our *oneness with Jesus*, as I had never known it before. But how to get faith strengthened? Not by striving after faith, but by *resting* on the Faithful One" (emphasis added).[2]

In Hebrews 12:2, Jesus is called the author and finisher of our faith. He begins it, and He perfects and finishes it. It really is "Who you know!" His name is Jesus!

As I was studying for this talk, I asked the Holy Spirit to bring order out of my chaos. There is so much scripture about faith, and I needed "a handle," like The Message said. As I meditated, I saw four categories of faith, and I could compare it to a baseball game (I know you men can identify with this.)

There is that "saving" faith that gets you to first base; then the "being" faith that moves you to second; the "serving" faith that takes you to third; and the "fighting" faith that brings you home.

First Base

Saving faith—faith for salvation. It is crucial to get your name in the Book. You do have to have a reservation before you leave earth! Remember when the seventy disciples went out and returned all excited? They had healed the sick, cast out demons. Then Jesus said, "Do not rejoice in this...but rather rejoice because your names are written in heaven" (Luke 10:17–20, NKJV). You cannot score a homerun unless you reach first base!

This faith to be born again, or be "saved," is a gift from God. "For by grace you have been saved through faith, and that not of yourselves; *it is* the gift of God, not of works, lest anyone should boast" (Eph. 2:8–9, NKJV).

Every man is given the measure of faith (Rom. 12:3), because it is not God's will that any should perish (2 Pet. 3:9).

And you know John 3:16: "For God so loved the world that he gave his only begotten Son, that whosoever (everybody is a "whosoever") believeth in him (Jesus) should not perish, but have everlasting life" (KJV).

But a gift must be received. I received Christ into my heart when I was thirteen, in a Sunday school assembly at the Hapeville Presbyterian Church. I felt that good warm feeling, just like John Wesley writes about. I knew I had done a very good thing. My part was to personally receive the gift my Lord was giving me—salvation, eternal life, and this life was in His Son.

Someone gave me a "starter" for Amish Bread, sometimes called Friendship Bread, together with a recipe. The starter was a gift, but every day I must follow the instructions. I knead it, work it with my hands (a good stress reliever); on the fifth day I add more to it (sugar, flour, and milk), then I knead it daily for five more days, and on the tenth day, I add a lot more stuff: flour, sugar, eggs, cinnamon, baking powder, baking soda, salt, oil, vanilla, and instant pudding mix. I can vary the flavor by my choice of mix. Someone once said that variety is the spice of life!

Then I divide the batter into four parts, give three away, and keep one starter for myself. My one portion that is left over in the bowl is then baked, and it yields two loaves. Most times I give one baked loaf to my family upstairs, because they smell it baking, and there is invariably an inquiring knock on my door.

Do you see how I received a gift, added to it, worked it, enjoyed its benefits, and had enough to pass on to three more people and double for me? Saving faith is a gift, and upon receipt, we follow the recipe (the Bible). You want to share it with others, to "Pass It On."

I was serving on a Lay Witness mission to St. James in Augusta, a grand traditional church, more than one hundred years old. The team was concerned because many members of the congregation kept saying proudly that they were on the cradle roll, but they didn't talk about a relationship with Jesus. The three team members assigned to a Sunday school class stressed salvation as a personal decision, and at the invitation, several in the class received the gift of salvation, asking Jesus to come into their hearts. They moved from the cradle roll to the Book of Life.

A conversion that meant the world to me and my family concerns my Bob. After our divorce, I continued to intercede in prayer for his salvation. In the fall of 2004, I felt in my spirit that something was happening and asked the Lord to let me know when it did. Bob telephoned from Mississippi shortly after that, asking me how to transfer his letter from our former church in Georgia. I questioned him, because he had said that Jesus was just a good man, not the Son of God. I led him through Romans 10:9–10 (NKJV):

> That if you confess with your mouth the Lord Jesus and believe in your heart that God has raised Him from the dead, you will be saved. For with the heart one believes unto righteousness, and with the mouth confession is made unto salvation.

And Verse 13:

> For *"whoever calls on the name of the Lord shall be saved"* (emphasis added).

Bob answered affirmatively, saying he wanted Jesus to forgive his sins and be his personal Lord and Savior; he prayed, inviting Jesus into his heart! The angels and I were rejoicing!

As we talked later, Bob went into more detail. He recalled that he was sitting in his chair one day, he thought about it, and he did it! Christ believed is Christ received!

It is a wonderful thing to have Christian parents and grandparents, to have that heritage, but their faith does not save you. They accepted their gift, and you must accept yours for yourself. There is nothing on earth more personal than your salvation.

My friend tells this story: A young boy made a boat. He carved it with his own hands, put on a sail and tied a string to it. He took the boat to a small lake in the local park, put it in the water, and was following along beside it when the string broke. The boat sailed away and he was unable to retrieve it. Sadly, he went home. Some days later he was passed by a toy store in town, and in the window he saw his boat! Excitedly he ran inside and told the owner that the boat belonged to him. The owner replied that the only way he could have the boat was to pay for it, and that would be five dollars. Sadly the boy returned home and emptied his piggy bank, but he didn't have five dollars. He did odd jobs for his parents and neighbors, and one day he had all the money. He ran to the store and purchased his own boat for five dollars. As he held it close to his heart he said, "Little boat, you are twice mine. I made you and I bought you!" In the same manner, we are twice God's: He made us and He bought us!

Second Base

Living faith. This is the faithfulness that has to do with our character, who we are when no one is looking. In Galatians 5:16, we are instructed to live by the Spirit, and in verse 22, we read, "the fruit of the Spirit is love, joy, peace, patience, kindness, goodness, *faithfulness*, gentleness and self-control" (NIV, emphasis added). These are the characteristics of Jesus. As we walk with Him, we become like Him.

Do you remember the television commercial that showed people with their pets? They looked like each other! Couples who have been married a long time tend to reflect each other. They can finish each other's sentences.

Many years ago (before Bob left), I was in the backyard of our home and I was singing a song to myself. Bob came in through the gate, singing the same song and he was at the same place!

Jesus promised that He would not leave us as orphans, but He would send another one, like Himself, the Holy Spirit. The Holy Spirit would live with us and be in us (John 14:15–20). He will transform us into the image of the dear Son, Jesus (2 Cor. 3:18). All the divinity of Christ was contained in one body, because He came to die. The Holy Spirit is in all believers; He is the one who led you to Christ. That is one of His main duties.

Jesus said in Acts 1:4–8 that we are to be filled with the *Holy Spirit, baptized in the Holy Spirit.* Then we receive *power* to witness for Jesus. This was not a suggestion but a command, and it is not difficult. The same way you received Christ, you receive the Holy Spirit. He is already in you! Just fully surrender and let Him fill you. In Luke 11:13, we read that even a bad father gives good gifts occasionally, so how much more will our heavenly Father give the Holy Spirit to those who ask?

In 1975, our goddaughter had come to live with us, and she turned my perfect little world upside down. I knelt at the altar of our church and prayed: "God, if you're real, show me, or I'm getting out of your church; I cannot cope." And then I heard Him speak to my spirit: "When in your life have things not worked out for you?"

My life passed before my eyes, like the drowning man, and I knew He was real and that He loved me; He had been there all the time. He filled me, from the bottom of my toes to the top of my head, like a thermometer on a hot day. He gave me that power to witness for Him, and to face what was ahead.

We are focusing right now on faithfulness as a fruit. Does an apple tree have to strain and sweat and grunt and groan to bear apples? It simply does what an apple tree does naturally—it bears apples. As a Spirit-filled believer, we don't have to strain and sweat, grunt, and groan to be faithful. We rest in the work of the Master Gardener as we abide in the vine. Jesus said, "I am the vine, you are the branches. He who abides in Me, and I in him, bears much fruit; for without Me you can do nothing" (John 15:5, NKJV). The fruit is on the branches; we simply stay connected to the Vine.

I remember my first foreign mission to Peru. Coming home all pumped up, my friend Linda and I made a covenant that we would be holy, and we would account to each other at the end of the day. Well, the harder we tried, the lousier we got. You see, we confused *being* with *doing*. We are called to *be* holy, even as He is holy (1 Pet. 1:16). It doesn't say to *do* holy. The doing comes from the being. We had to surrender to the work of the

Holy Spirit in us, just resting in Him and His faithfulness and letting Him work through us.

Dr. Helen Roseveare writes: "In the great realm of life—abundant, full living, there is obviously so much beyond the five senses, and the measurements and definitions of science. Here, faith is the active force, the sixth sense.[3] So, as Spirit-filled Christians, we do not have just five senses, but six! It is just as natural for us to have faith come forth as it is to see, hear, taste, smell and touch. Faith is a part of who we are in Christ!

When the storms come, and the testings and the trials bump us, we spill what we are full of—*faith*!

In the account of David's battle with Goliath in 1 Samuel 17:37: "David said, 'The Lord, who delivered me from the paw of the lion and from the paw of the bear, He will deliver me from the hand of the Philistines'" (NKJV). The point here is that time and again God had rescued David, and this was just another one of those times—naturally! God did it before, He'd do it again, and, of course, He did!

I confess that I have really been stressed about being a speaker here today. My heart is to bless my Lord and be used by Him to bless you as well. I knew James would be awesome, and I wanted to live up to the faith that Walt and the Methodist Men had in me. So I was tensed up, typing away at my computer, and my neck just froze on me. I am really not into pain; I just don't suffer that well; I have a low tolerance. That evening, as I was journaling, I found myself writing: "You are being tested." Duh! Of course!

And then I just got still, and I knew. "Be still and know that I *am* God" (Ps. 46:10, KJV). My faith is in the faithfulness of my Lord Jesus; when He calls, He equips. I went to my dresser mirror and spoke out loud to myself the same words I heard when the Holy Spirit filled me in 1975: "When in your life have things not worked out for you?"

They have always worked out for me and they will this time, too. You see before you today a clinging vine; I'm letting the Spirit flow. It's like we say on mission trips: Glow with the Flow!

Third Base

Serving faith. Love must have an object. You cannot love and not do something; our love must be expressed, just as the Father's love was expressed in Jesus (John 3:16).

This serving faith is a ministry gift of the Holy Spirit. See 1 Corinthians 12:7–9: "Now to each one the manifestation of the Spirit is given for the common good. To one there is given through the Spirit the message of wisdom, to another the message of knowledge by means of the same Spirit, to another *faith* by the same Spirit" (NIV, emphasis added). The Life Application Bible has this notation with reference to verse 9: "All Christians have faith. Some, however, have the gift of faith, which is an *unusual measure of trust in the Holy Spirit's power*"(emphasis added).

We are focusing on the ministry gift of faith. We see that it is given for the good of all, to build up the Body of Christ—to serve.

Jesus said that He did not come to *be* served, but *to* serve (Matt. 20:28), and when Peter was describing Jesus, he said "who went about doing good" (Acts 10:38, KJV). Therefore, to be imitators of Christ, we must be "do-gooders." It's not because you have to, but you want to; you get to!

Leo Buscaglia says: "Your life is a gift from God, but what you do with it is your gift back to Him."[4]

Paul says in Eph. 2:10: "we are his workmanship, created in Christ Jesus to do good works, which God prepared in advance for us to do" (NIV). This is mind-blowing news—that before we were a glimmer in our earthly father's eyes, God had plans for us! We have assignments to accomplish!

I tell you one thing—I never dreamed I would be an author, much less a public speaker. Doesn't that beat all? His plans for us are so good!

God will take your availability and infuse it with His ability. That way He gets the glory! We have His promise that those He calls, He equips because He won't let you be ashamed or embarrassed (2 Tim. 1:11–12, KJV).

The apostle James tells us that faith without works is dead. I received a revelation of this one day as I was pulling out of my driveway on my way to church. Right there on Peters Road was a dead possum; apparently someone had run over it. In the South we say "road kill." It was a possum, yes; but it was dead. There was no life in it; it wasn't good for anything. In a day or two it was going to stink. The only ones who would benefit from this dead possum would be the scavengers.

Our faith is like that—it does not benefit the Kingdom of God unless it is used; has life in it! James continues in Chapter 2:20–22: "You foolish man, do you want evidence that faith without deeds is useless? Was not our ancestor Abraham considered righteous for what he did when he offered his son Isaac on the altar? You see that *his faith and his actions were working together, and his faith was made complete by what he did"* (NIV, emphasis added).

Wow! Our faith is perfected, brought to maturity, completed by our actions! But that's not all; there is another astounding scripture in Hebrews 5:8–9: "Though he was God's Son, he learned trusting-obedience by what he suffered, *just as we do.* Then, having arrived at the full stature of his maturity and having been announced by God as high priest in the order of Melchizedek, he became the source of eternal salvation to all who believingly (faithfully) obey him" (THE MESSAGE, emphasis added).

In an interview, I heard Billy Graham respond to a reporter's question about the thing he wanted most. He replied, "To hear God say, 'Well done, thou good and faithful servant.'" Me, too!

Fourth: Home Base

Fighting faith. We're getting close to home and the battle intensifies. The enemy does not want us to make it to the end; he comes to steal, kill, rob and destroy (John 10:10). We need "fighting" faith. Paul talks about the "good fight of faith." He says that we wrestle with wicked spirits, and he gives some basic instructions:

> Finally, my brethren, be strong in the Lord, and in the *power of His might.* Put on the whole armor of God, that you may be able to stand against the wiles of the devil. For we do not wrestle against flesh and blood, but against principalities, against powers, against the rulers of the darkness of this age, against spiritual hosts of wickedness in the heavenly places. Therefore, take up the whole armor of God, that you may be able to withstand in the evil day, and having done all to *stand, stand* therefore, having girded your waist with truth, and having put on the breastplate of righteousness, and having shod your feet with the preparation of the gospel of peace; *above all,* taking the shield of *faith,* with which you shall be able to quench *all* the fiery darts of the wicked one. And take the helmet of salvation, and the sword of the Spirit, which is the Word of God; praying…being watchful.
> —Ephesians 6:10-18, nkjv, emphasis added

Note that we are commanded to stand. "Having done all to stand, stand." There is no time element here. You don't stand an hour, a day, a month, a year; you stand to the end, until your victory is manifested.

Some of my skirmishes with the devil have been short-term, as he conceded his defeat right away, but others took a little more time. God's promise of reconciliation and restoration between Bob and me took thirty years, but it was well worth the "standing" and those in-between years were not wasted!

In the Greek, the definition of "stand" is to "hold your ground." We recently celebrated the resurrection of our Lord Jesus Christ; the Father proclaimed Him victor over the whole realm of darkness. Jesus is seated at the right hand of the Father, and the church (that's us) is to hold the ground that He has given to us. He said the gates of hell would not prevail against us (Matt. 16:18). This is a picture of the enemy attacking to try to take what is rightfully ours through Christ.

However, the church does more than withstand assaults; it advances against them, which is why Satan and his evil forces try so hard to bring down the church and its leaders. He also targets families, and tries to take away our children.

When we fight with the attitude of getting the victory, we are relinquishing what we already have in Christ Jesus. I believe it's Joel Osteen who preaches that we are victors, not victims. In Deuteronomy 28:7, the Lord says that He will cause the enemy that comes against us one way to "flee seven ways," and in verse 13, He says that we are "the head, and not the tail."

There is a great story that is attributed to Smith Wigglesworth, a preacher of great faith. (It certainly goes along with his reputation.) He had retired for the night but woke up when he heard a sound in the next room. He went in and saw Satan rocking back and forth in a rocking chair. Smith said to him, "Oh, it's just you," and went back to bed.

These weapons of our warfare are defensive, with the exception of the Sword of the Spirit, which is the Word of God; it can be used both defensively and offensively. These weapons do not cover our backs, because we are standing our ground. There is a popular television commercial featuring Shaq, the 7'1" NBA basketball player. It says, "Shaq's got your back!" Christians can do much better than that because we have the Lord God almighty as our rear-guard (Isa. 52:12, NKJV)!

There is defensive armor for every point of attack by the enemy: the helmet to protect the mind, the breast-plate to protect the vital organs in your chest (heart, lungs), the girdle to protect your belly and reproductive organs, and the shoes—these feet that do the walking, but *above all, take up the shield of faith* wherewith you are able to quench all the fiery darts of the wicked!

When God says "all," does He mean 50 percent, 75 percent, 80 percent, etc.? He says what He means, and He means what He says. All is all—100 percent. All the fiery darts!

I read once that the shield the Roman soldiers used was notched, so that they could link on to each other and form a wall. This is a picture of the church, where we join with our brothers and sisters-in-Christ, as a united wall to resist the enemy attacks. The shield was also coated so that the darts would be immediately extinguished upon contact.

We have the weapons we need, but the most important thing is that we "be strong in the Lord and in the power of His might" (Eph. 6:10). In Ephesians 1:19,

Paul said he was praying that we would know "the exceeding greatness of his power in us who believe (have faith; that's you and me) according to the working of *His mighty power*" (emphasis added).

He goes on to say in verses 20–22 that "Jesus is set far above all principality, and power, and might, and dominion, and every name that is named, not only in this world but in that which is to come, and has put all things under his feet." All things are under His feet; therefore, when we are in Christ Jesus, they are under our feet as well.

Didn't God say back in the beginning (Gen. 3:15) that the seed of woman (that's Messiah, Jesus) would bruise Satan's head? Jesus has His feet on the neck of Satan.

We do not fight *for* victory; we fight *from* victory! Our power comes from our position in Christ. "This is the victory that overcomes the world, even our faith" (1 John 5:4, NIV).

Let's review: This "saving" faith that got us to first base is focused on what Jesus did for us on the cross, His body and His blood. He paid the price for our redemption.

The "living" faith, moving us on to second, is a fruit of the Spirit, whereby we are transformed, from glory to glory, into the image of Christ.

The "serving" faith gets us to third, making us imitators of Christ, His agents on earth at such a time as this to advance His kingdom.

Through the "fighting" faith, we are "more than

conquerors in Christ Jesus" (Rom. 8:37). We don't just win; we get the "booty."

"How To Be Faith-full In A Faith-less World And Develop Your Faith God's Way" can be condensed into one word, one name: *Jesus*! He is the Way, the Truth, the Life, the Author and the Finisher of our faith.

Hold tight to Him, and *never let go*! It will be quite a run, and you will arrive at home—*safe*!

Recipe for Amish Bread

Day 1: Do nothing if this is the day you receive your batter. (Note date on the bag.)

Day 2: Mush bag

Day 3: Mush bag

Day 4: Mush bag

Day 5: Mush bag

Day 6: Add to bag: 1 cup of flour, 1 cup of sugar, 1 cup of milk. Mush bag.

Day 7: Mush bag

Day 8: Mush bag

Day 9: Mush bag

Day 10: Follow the instructions below:

> Pour entire contents of bag into a *non-metal* bowl. Add following ingredients:
> 1-1/2 cups flour
> 1-1/2 cups sugar
> 1-1/2 cups milk.

> Measure out 4 separate batters of one (1) cup each into 4 one-gallon Ziploc bags. (You will have some batter left over in your bowl.) Keep one of the bags for yourself, and give the other

three to friends, along with a copy of the directions and recipe.

Preheat the oven to 325 degrees.

To the remaining batter, add:
    3 eggs
    1 cup oil
    1 cup sugar
    ½ cup of milk
    2 tsp. cinnamon
    ½ tsp. vanilla
    1-1/2 tsp. baking powder
    l/2 tsp. baking soda
    1/2 tsp. salt
    2 cups flour
    1 large box instant vanilla pudding (or flavor
of your choice)

Grease two loaf pans (9 ¼ x 5 ¼ x 2 ¾) and mix additional 1/2 cup of sugar and 1/2 tsp. of cinnamon into a small bowl. Dust the greased pans with *half* of the mixture.

Pour batter evenly into the two pans and sprinkle the remaining sugar/cinnamon mix on top.

Bake 50–60 minutes. It is done when inserted toothpick comes out clean.

Cool until loaf loosens from pan, about ten minutes. Turn on to serving dish. Serve warm or cold.

If you keep a starter for yourself, you will be baking every ten days. The bread is very good and makes a great gift. Only the Amish know how to create a starter, so if you give them all away, you will have to wait until someone gives you one back.

Enjoy my friend! God bless!

Chapter Five

The Power of a Virtuous Woman:
Accessing the Goodness of God

*I*AM BREATHING A sigh of relief now, because the first session is over and I did not die! The next session after lunch will be divided into the men and women, and of course, I get the women! That's just the way it is. I suppose I enjoy speaking to women because "I am one!" I am always uplifted by their strength, courage and to put it bluntly, their "guts!" God gave women an extraordinary ability to endure, and it is an awesome builder of faith to be in their presence and share their testimonies of grace. They are overcomers with a capital "O!"

The Message

I heard this joke: these three men were hiking in the woods when they came to a river they needed to cross. The first man prayed, "Lord, give me big muscles so I can swim across," and the Lord gave him muscles like Popeye. He swam across the river and it took about an hour.

The second man prayed, "Lord, give me strength and a boat." The Lord answered his prayer, and he sailed across in about forty minutes.

The third man prayed, "Lord, turn me into a woman," so the Lord did. She took out a map, went a short distance to the bridge, and walked across. It took her about ten minutes!

There is an account in the fifth chapter of Mark about a miracle Jesus performed on the way to another miracle. I had a revelation when I read this many years ago, and it changed my life. Since that time, I constantly pray, "Lord, please make me a virtuous, godly woman." I'll show you why.

In Mark 5:21–42 (KJV), we read:

> And when Jesus was passed over again by ship unto the other side, much people gathered unto him; and he was nigh unto the sea. And, behold, there cometh one of the rulers of the synagogue, Jairus by name; and when he saw him, he fell at his feet, And besought him greatly, saying, My little daughter lieth at the point of death: *I pray thee*, come and lay hands on her, that she may be healed; and

she shall live. And Jesus went with him, and much people followed him, and thronged him. And a certain woman, which had an issue of blood twelve years, and had suffered many things of many physicians, and had spent all she had, and was nothing bettered, but rather grew worse, when she had heard of Jesus, came in the press behind, and touched his garment. For she said, If I may touch but his clothes, I shall be whole. And straightway the fountain of her blood dried up; and she felt in her body that she was healed of that plague. And Jesus, immediately knowing in himself that virtue had gone out of him, turned him about in the press, and said, Who touched my clothes? And his disciples said unto him, Thou seest the multitude thronging thee, and sayest thou, Who touched me? And he looked round about to see her that had done this thing. But the woman fearing and trembling, knowing what was done in her, came and fell down before him, and told him all the truth. And he said unto her, daughter, thy faith hath made thee whole; go in peace, and be whole of thy plague. While he yet spoke, there came from the ruler of the synagogue's house certain which said, Thy daughter is dead: why troublest thou the Master any further? As soon as Jesus heard the word that was spoken, he saith unto the ruler of the synagogue, Be not afraid, only believe. And he suffered no man to follow him, save Peter, and James, and John the brother of James. And he cometh to the house of the ruler of the synagogue, and seeth the tumult, and them that wept and wailed greatly. And when he was come in, he saith unto them, Why make this ado, and weep? The damsel is not dead, but sleepeth. And they laughed him to scorn. But when he had put them all out, he taketh the father and the mother of the damsel, and them that were him, and entereth in where the damsel was lying. And he took the damsel by the hand, and said unto her, Talitha, cumi, which is being interpreted, Damsel, I say unto thee, arise. And straightway the damsel arose, and walked; for she was of the age of twelve years. And they were astonished with a great astonishment.

These two miracles had something in common: *faith!* Jairus said in verse 23 that if Jesus would come and lay hands on his daughter, she would be healed and she would live. Note that he was one of the rulers of the synagogue, and the religious leaders at that time were not too happy about Jesus, so Jairus was bucking the top brass, risking excommunication.

The woman in verse 28 said that if she could just touch his clothes, the hem of His garment, she would be healed. They both said what they believed, and they received their miracles.

Jesus said in Mark 9:23: "If you can believe, all things are possible to him who believes" (NKJV). And in Mark 11:22–23: "Have faith in God. For verily I say unto you, That whosoever shall *say* to this mountain, Be thou removed, and be thou cast into the sea, and shall not doubt in his heart, but shall believe (*have faith*) that those things he *says* shall come to pass, he shall have whatsoever he *says*" (NKJV, emphasis added).

Our problem is that we *pray*, and then we *say*, and our saying and our praying don't stay in agreement, so we get double-minded, and the double-minded man does not get anything from the Lord (James 1:7–8).

Have you ever prayed for someone, and they get right up and knock down everything for which you prayed by their words? ("Well, I hope so; well, if it's God's will; it always rains when we go on vacation; I just knew something like this would happen, it always does.") They are really saying they don't believe God will do it for them; that His Word is true. I have prayed for myself and done the same thing!

In Isaiah 1:18, the Lord says: "Come now, and let us reason together." In other words, present your case (NKJV).

I worked for lawyers for forty-five years, and we did not go before the judge without sufficient evidence and case law. What does the law say; what are the precedents (previous judgments based on the law)? This was the foundation of our case. Our Judge is God Himself, and our case law is the Holy Bible.

In this instance, we have two people in great distress, and they are coming to Jesus for rescue and relief. They are "reasoning" with Him, and giving us another "precedent" on which to base our petitions today.

As to the woman with the issue of blood, Mark 5:25

says that she had been bleeding for twelve years, so we know she was unclean.

Leviticus 15:25–27 (NIV) says:

> When a woman has a discharge of blood for many days at a time other than her monthly period or has a discharge that continues beyond her period, she will be unclean as long as she has the discharge, just as in the days of her period. Any bed she lies on while her discharge continues will be unclean, as is her bed during the monthly period, and anything she sits on will be unclean, as during her period. Whoever touches them will be unclean; he must wash his clothes and bathe with water, and he will be unclean till evening .

Verse 31 says:

> You must keep the Israelites separate from things that make them unclean.

Anyone she touched would be unclean, and anyone who touched her would be unclean; she was not supposed to be in public. If she had a husband, he could not have relations with her because then he also would be unclean. She could not go to the synagogue or to the temple. Just think of how isolated she was; how lonely she must have been. All her money was gone; she was hopeless and surely very depressed.

Also, she was physically depleted. Can you imagine bleeding heavily for twelve years? Many years ago my doctor put me on a hormone replacement, and I bled for three months. I would get off the train, take the escalator to get to my job, and just hang onto the railing because I was so weak. I stopped taking that medication—enough was enough!

This poor woman had seen many doctors, but was no better than when she started. She was desperate and at the end of her rope, and so was Jairus. Then she heard about Jesus. No doubt the news was spreading like wildfire—all the healings, the miracles He was performing. Could this be the Messiah? Faith welled up inside her.

> Now faith is (present tense) the substance (ground of, confidence) of things hoped for, the evidence of things not seen.
>
> —HEBREWS 11:1, NKJV

Back to Mark 5:27–28:

> She came in the press (crowd) behind, and touched his garment, for she said, If I may touch his clothes I shall be whole.

The King James Version says "garment" and "clothes," while other translations say "cloak" or "robe." The New Believer says, "the fringe of His robe." The King James in Matthew 9:20 refers to the "hem of his garment," and Luke 8:44 says, "the border of his garment."

Turn now to Numbers 15:37–41 (NKJV):

> Again the Lord spoke to Moses, saying, "Speak
> to the children of Israel: Tell them to make tas-
> sels on the corners of their garments throughout
> their generations, and to put a blue thread in the
> tassels of the corners. And you shall have the
> tassel, that you my look upon it and remember
> all the commandments of the Lord and do
> them, and that you may not follow the harlotry
> to which your own heart and your own eyes
> are inclined, and that you may remember and
> do all My commandments and be holy for your
> God. I am the Lord your God, who brought you
> out of the land of Egypt, to be your God: I am
> the Lord your God."

This is the tallith, or prayer shawl. We still see these garments worn by Jewish men today, especially while praying at the Western Wall in Jerusalem. It is a rectangular garment with tassels (fringes) at the four corners, representing the four corners of the earth, and they are sewed on with ribbons of blue.

Dake's Annotated Reference Bible goes into more depth: "Tradition maintains that the threads of the tassels were white to symbolize righteousness, that there was a conspicuous blue thread among them to symbolize the commandments were of heavenly origin, and that the arrangements of the threads and knots were of great importance, because they symbolized the 613 precepts which the law was believed to contain...one thing is certain, when they saw the fringes or tassels, they were reminded of the law and their responsibility to obey it, and their calling to be a holy people unto

Jehovah...In Christ's time the Pharisees enlarged their fringes hoping thereby to prove their great piety (Matt. 23:5)."[5]

Don't miss verse 41: "I AM the Lord your God!"

When Moses was told by God to go to Pharaoh and tell him to let his people go, Moses asked God what to answer when he was asked, "What is his name?" And God answered, "I AM THAT I AM" (Exod. 3:13–14, KJV). In the Gospel of John, it is interesting to see how many times Jesus referred to himself as "I AM." He said: "I am the bread; I am the life, I am the vine, I am the way; I am the truth, I am the life," and "before Abraham was I am."

After the resurrection, the disciples had gone fishing, but they had caught nothing (John 21:3). Jesus was on the shore and yelled to them to cast their nets on the right side of the ship. When they did, the net was full of great fish. They counted a total of 153. In Hebrew, numbers have equivalent letters, and the number 153 translates, "I am God."

Malachi, prophesying about the coming of the Lord (4:2, NKJV) says: "But unto you who fear my name the Sun of Righteousness shall arise with healing in His wings." Through this miracle of healing the woman with the issue of blood, Jesus is again affirming that he is deity; he is Messiah. We don't have to struggle with translations —whether garments, robes, cloaks, or a tallith—she touched Jesus and all that He represented—the I AM! We can get so caught up in the gifts that we miss the giver.

> Upon touching Jesus, right away the fountain of
> her blood dried up, and she felt in her body that
> she was healed of that plague.
> —Mark 5:29, kjv

As a woman, you know when you are bleeding like that; you feel it flowing from you. How many times have you felt panicky; that the blood is coming through your clothes and everyone will know! She *felt* it stop!

Verse 30 is dynamite: "And Jesus immediately knowing in himself that virtue had gone out of him." There is an account beginning in Luke 6:17, where Jesus had come down from the mountain after naming the twelve disciples. There was a huge crowd; He was healing them of their diseases and delivering them from unclean spirits (kjv). In verse 19: "And the whole multitude sought to touch him; for there went virtue out of him, and healed them all."

The definition of the word *virtue* in *Vine's Expository Dictionary of New Testament Words* reads: "moral goodness, virtue, renown, excellence or praise, the manifestation of His divine power, where virtue is enjoined as an essential quality in the exercise of faith."[6]

Look at Mark 5:30–33 again: "And Jesus, immediately knowing in himself that virtue had gone out of him, turned him about in the press, and said, Who touched my clothes? And his disciples said unto him, You see the multitude thronging you, and you say, Who touched me? And he looked round about to see her that had done this thing. But the woman, fearing and trembling, knowing what was done in her, came and fell down before Him, and told him all the truth" (KJV).

Jesus knew he had been touched, and it was not just a physical touch. He was in a crowd and being touched by a lot of people, but this was a different touch—not physical, but spiritual. She was making a demand on his deity, the I AM. There had to be many in that crowd who needed healing, but they did not make a claim on His virtue, His power.

The previous definition of *virtue* in *Vine's* bears repeating: "Virtue is enjoined as an essential quality in the exercise of faith." *The power and the faith are partners*! He could not hold back the power, because of His goodness, His moral excellence, His integrity. And, of course, He did not want to hold back His power. Our faith works because of God's pledge to us that He will honor his word. When you join faith with the power of His goodness, you get a miracle.

Mother Julian of Norwich wrote:

> To know the goodness of God is the highest prayer of all, and it is a prayer that accommodates itself to our most lowly needs. It quickens our soul, and vitalizes it, developing it in grace and virtue...Our lover (Jesus) desires indeed that our soul should cleave to him with all its might, and ever hold on to his goodness.[7]

Jesus now speaks to the woman (Mark 5:34): "Daughter, your faith has made you *whole*, go in peace, and be *whole* of your plague" (emphasis added). Jesus addresses her as "Daughter." She is a member of the family of God, no longer an outcast. Her faith has made her whole, not just physically but spiritually. She was healed body, soul (her mind, will and emotions) and spirit. He gives her shalom, peace; her healing is complete!

But Jesus is not finished; this is a miracle on the way to a miracle. Jairus had come first and Jesus had not forgotten him. Continuing in Mark 5:35–36 (KJV): "While Jesus yet spoke, there came from the ruler of the synagogue's *house* (Jairus' house) *certain* which said, Thy daughter is dead, why trouble thou the Master any further? As soon as Jesus heard the *word that was spoken*, he saith unto the ruler of the synagogue (Jairus), Be not afraid, only believe" (emphasis added).

Note the conflict here between the servant's words and Jairus' words. The servant said that the girl was dead, but Jairus had said that if Jesus would come and lay hands on her, she would be healed and she would live. Jesus did not give Jairus an opportunity to speak again. He simply said, "Do not be afraid, only believe."

Fear blocks faith; they cannot co-exist. I once read that there are 365 "fear nots" in the Bible, one for each day of the year.

In verse 37, "And he (Jesus) suffered no man to follow him, except Peter, James and John." He did not want any negative followers. You know, there are attic people and basement people. Choose your companions wisely, especially when you need a miracle.

Continuing in verses 38–41: "And he comes to...

(Jairus' house) and sees the tumult, and them that wept and wailed greatly (the professional mourners), and then He came in and said to them, Why are you making this ado, and weep? The damsel is not dead, but sleeps. And they laughed him to scorn. (Easy to turn sorrow into laughter when the sorrow is not real.) But when he had put them all out, he took the father and the mother of the damsel, and them that were with him (Peter, James and John) and entered in where the damsel was lying, and he took the damsel by the hand, and said unto her, Talitha cumi, which is, being interpreted, Damsel, I say unto you, arise." (In Aramaic, "damsel" means "little girl.")

Another interesting side note here is that the custom would have been to wrap the child's body in a prayer shawl, so literally Jesus said to her, "Little girl, wrapped in the Word, arise!"

Verse 42 continues, "And straightway the damsel arose, and walked, for she was of the age of twelve years."

When this little girl was born, the woman with the issue of blood started bleeding. They were both healed the same day! This little girl's daddy, Jairus, put his faith in Jesus; he never left Jesus' side. He was cleaving to the goodness of God, just like the woman. And he got what he said—his daughter was made whole.

I mentioned that I experienced a personal revelation of this scripture (rhema), and it became very special to me. Several years ago my sister-in-law, Barbara, asked me to pray for a young man named Bruce. He had a football scholarship and was about to leave for college, but he developed leukemia, and it was the fast kind. Of course, he was devastated, as was his family. I felt such a heavy burden to pray for Bruce; I could not get him off my mind, so I continued to intercede. One day as I was driving to work, I reached out in my spirit and touched the hem of Jesus' garment. A great peace (shalom) came over me, and I knew Bruce was healed, so I started praising the Lord right there in my car! That evening Barbara telephoned and said, "You can't guess what has happened," and I replied, "Bruce has been healed." She asked, "How did you know?" and I told her about touching the hem of Jesus' garment that morning.

Do you see the awesomeness of this? We, as women (and men) of faith have an intimate relationship with Jesus that enables us to touch the hem of His garment! Our God will not withhold His power, but will flow into us, and through us into others, to bring healing and wholeness.

Peter takes us even deeper into this revelation in 2 Peter 1:3–4 (KJV, emphasis added): "According as his divine power (the power of the Holy Spirit) hath given unto us *all* things that *pertain* to life and godliness, through the knowledge of him that hath called us to glory and *virtue*, whereby are given unto us exceeding great and precious promises; that by these ye might be partakers of the divine nature, having escaped the corruption that is in the world though lust."

Don't miss this: We have *exceeding great and precious*

promises (His Word); we are *partakers* of his divine nature! Continuing in verses 5 through 7: "And beside this, giving all diligence, add to your faith virtue, and to virtue knowledge, and to knowledge, temperance, and to temperance patience, and to patience godliness, and to godliness brotherly kindness, and to brotherly kindness charity (love)."

Here again we see that faith and virtue are partners, going hand-in-hand. There is a progression in our walk; we are maturing.

"For if these things be in you, and abound, *they make you that* you shall neither *be* barren nor unfruitful in the knowledge of our Lord Jesus Christ."

We won't be barren or unfruitful because we are getting to know Jesus better and better, and are becoming more and more like Him.

"But he that lacketh these things is blind, and cannot see afar off, and has forgotten that he was purged from his old sins, wherefore the rather, brethren (and sisters), give diligence to make your calling and election sure: for if ye do these things, you *shall never fall*"(v. 10, emphasis added).

Ladies and gentlemen, we are not blind and we have not forgotten what Christ did for us, and what He has brought us to; and don't you love that part? *You shall never fall!*"

When Peter was describing Jesus to Cornelius and his household (Acts 10:38, KJV), he said:

> How God anointed Jesus of Nazareth with the
> Holy Ghost and with power; who went about

doing good, and healing all that were oppressed
by the devil, for God was with him .

That's us! We have been anointed, set apart; we have
an intimate relationship with Jesus; we have the power
of the Holy Spirit; and we are to go about doing good,
healing all who are oppressed by the devil, for God is
with us!

We have access to His virtue, the power of His goodness, and we shall not fall!

Because God said *so*!

Chapter Six

Don't Hang in There—Stand on the Promises of God:
Applying the Promises of God

OLLOWING THE MESSAGE at the ladies' session, there was sweet ministry. I had brought a prayer shawl and used it as an illustration during the teaching. As always, there were many needs so we sat those who wanted prayer in a chair, wrapped them in the prayer shawl and anointed them with oil. The ladies, as the Spirit led, laid hands on their sisters and interceded on their behalf. We touched the hem of Jesus' garment and His virtue flowed upon us, through us and in us. You could sense God's pleasure as His daughters partnered with the Holy Spirit that afternoon, "doing good!"

Pastor James blessed us even more with the next combined session, and then it was supper time. Christians know how to put on the feed bag, and there was more sweet fellowship during our meal.

Now it was time for my last teaching, preparing the ground for James to close. I am always nervous, and frankly hope that will always be the case, so that in my weakness I will be dynamite for Jesus, because He has to do the work (2 Cor. 12: 9–10) and that way He gets the glory!

The Message

A friend of mine knew I was going through a difficult time and she asked me how I was doing. My reply, "I'm hanging in there." She rebuked me, "You don't just hang in there; you stand on the promises!" I have never ever since that time claimed that I was "hanging in there" because she is right.

Can you get a mental picture of that in your mind? You have the Word of God, His promises under you as a firm foundation, but you are up above, holding onto this rope, and you are swinging from one side to the other. Faith is one side, and doubt is on the other, so you just swing. Now I believe; now I don't.

Poor thing! Your swinging is futile because double-minded people don't get anything from the Lord (James 1:7–8).

God does not want His children hanging; He wants them standing. Remember our teaching this morning about being "faith-full," and how we put on the whole armor of God? Having done all to stand, we stand on the firm foundation of the Word, which changes not.

We have a heavenly Father who is omniscient, omnipresent, and omnipotent. That means He knows everything, He is always present, and He is all powerful—the Lord God Almighty. He has a lot to say, to teach us, and knowing His children, He wrote it down. Our lives really are open-book tests.

The Lord speaks in Isaiah. 55:11: "So shall My word be that goes forth from My mouth. It shall not return to Me void, but it shall accomplish what I please, and it shall prosper *in the thing* for which I sent it" (NKJV). God is saying: Because I said so! That settles it!

John opens his gospel (John 1:1, 14): "In the beginning was the Word, and the Word was with God, and the Word was God...And the Word became flesh and dwelt among us" (NKJV).

In Hebrews 1:2–3, 10, we read how Jesus spoke the worlds into existence by His Word; that He formed the foundation of the earth, and everything is being upheld by the Word of His power. Jesus and the Word are one. The nature of the Word is miraculous; the Word is a living thing.

> For the word of God is living and powerful, and sharper than any two-edged sword, piercing even to the dividing asunder of soul and spirit, and of joints and marrow, and is a discerner of the thoughts and intents of the heart.
>
> —HEBREWS 4:12, NKJV

We are born again by the Word: "Having been born again, not of corruptible seed, but incorruptible, through the word of God which lives and abides forever" (1 Pet. 1:23, NKJV).

This scripture is very real to me. When my husband left, after confessing his indiscretions, I felt very dirty. My marriage bed had been defiled. As I was praying for forgiveness, the Lord spoke to my spirit: "You are born of incorruptible seed; nothing from the outside entering in can contaminate you. You are pure and holy in My sight." Because God said so, and I agreed with His Word, His truth set me free.

Satan wants to keep us in bondage with his lies, but Jesus came to set the captives free. He says: "And you shall know the truth, and the truth shall make you free" (John 8.32, NKJV).

The miracle action of the Word is released through our words (agreeing with God), and through our actions.

Paul says: "The word is near you, in your mouth and in your heart (that is, the word of faith which we preach)" (Rom. 10:8, NKJV). He is quoting here excerpts from an address by Moses to the Israelites in Deut. 30, urging them to return to God.

In the Book of Wisdom, Proverbs (4:20–23), we are instructed: "My son, give attention to my words; incline your ear to my sayings, do not let them depart from your eyes; keep them in the midst of your heart; for they are life to those who find them, and health to all their flesh. Keep your heart with all diligence, for out of it *spring* the issues of life" (NKJV).

Jesus stressed the importance of the Word in the granddaddy of all the parables, the Parable of the Sower, Mark 4:1–20. In verse 13, He tells the disciples that they need to know and understand this parable in order to grasp all the others, because Jesus taught in parables.

Follow along with me in verses 3–8: "Listen! Behold, a sower went out to sow. And it happened, as he sowed, that some seed fell by the wayside; and the birds of the air came and devoured it. Some fell on stony ground, where it did not have much earth; and immediately it sprang up because it had no depth of earth. But when the sun was up it was scorched, and because it had no root it withered away. And some seed fell among thorns; and the thorns grew up and choked it, and it yielded no crop. But other seed fell on good ground and yielded a crop that sprang up, increased and produced: some thirtyfold, some sixty, and some a hundred" (NKJV).

When they were alone, the disciples asked the meaning of the parable. In verses 14–15, Jesus explains: "The sower sows the word. And these are the ones by the wayside where the word is sown. When they hear, Satan comes immediately and takes away the word that was sown in their hearts."

The Word is crucial to our lives and the enemy knows it. In the seed is the image of the whole—all we can be, our potential.

Jesus further teaches in verses 16–17: "These likewise are the ones sown on stony ground who, when they hear the word, immediately receive it with gladness; and they have no root in themselves, and so endure only for a time. Afterward, when tribulation or persecution rises for the word's sake, immediately they stumble (are offended)." If you have no root, you will not stand.

During an ice storm in Georgia, it is the pine that falls because its taproot goes straight down. Over it goes under the weight of the ice. Afflictions and persecutions come; you can count on it, and often people get offended.

> A brother offended *is harder to win* than a strong city, and contentions *are* like the bars of a castle.
> —PROVERBS 18:19, NKJV

We have folks coming in the front door of the church, and others going out the back door, carrying their offenses with them. Evelyn, who served on many missions and was a dear friend of mine, claimed her constant prayer was: "Lord, give me a hide like a water buffalo!" Amen to that!

Continuing in Mark 4:18–19: "Now these are the ones sown among thorns; they are the ones who hear the word, and the cares of this world, the deceitfulness of riches, and the desires (lusts) for other things entering in choke the word, and it becomes unfruitful."

If you know anything about gardening, you know

how thorns and weeds can choke out your good plants, causing them to wither and die. Jesus lists three thorns, which are (1) cares of the world. That's our worries and anxieties, such as paying the bills, putting the kids through school, keeping food on the table, just life in general; (2) deceitfulness of riches. We go for the "big bucks" because we believe if we have enough money, we have no problems, which is a big lie of the enemy; and (3) desires (lusts) for other things. Lust is a perversion of love; lust is "what's in it for me?" while love is "what's in it for the other person?" These "enter in" because we let our guard down. We don't have on our full armor, especially that shield of faith to knock down *all* the fiery darts of the enemy (Eph. 6:10–18).

In these seven verses where Jesus is teaching the disciples the meaning of this master parable of the sower, note that in every verse the "Word" is mentioned. If you see something once or twice, take notice, but seven times? It's important, major!

We learn in Romans 10:17 that "faith comes by hearing, and hearing by the word of God," and from Hebrews 11:6, we know that "without faith (believing in God's Word), it is impossible to please Him."

Jesus has more to say about the Word in John 15:1, 3, and 7: "I am the true vine, and My Father is the vine-dresser…You are already clean because of the word (the washing of the Word) which I have spoken to you…If you abide in Me, and My words abide in you, you will ask what you desire, and it shall be done for you" (NKJV).

The Word must abide, make its habitation, take up

residence in our hearts, so that we are not moved by circumstances, but only by the Word.

Get your answer before you pray by finding out what the Lord has to say in His Word about your situation. Get His Word into you, then stand on it, say it, pray it, and keep saying and praying the Word until it is manifested. It may take awhile, because spiritual things take time, but it will come, and it will come in God's way and in the fullness of His time.

My sister-in-law and I sat down by a little pond in my back yard, and we held hands and prayed in agreement that Bob (her twin brother, my husband) would be saved and come home. We knew we were praying God's will because His Word says that His will is that none should perish, and He is a reconciling God. Also, I had God's promise of restoration. We persevered, staying in agreement no matter how the circumstances appeared, and after thirty years the answer came.

When you are praying for someone's salvation, there is the matter of free will. Ruth Bell Graham wrote:

> If a nest of wild hornets were left in the room,
> And the creatures allowed to go free,
> They would not compel you against your will,
> They'd just make you willing to flee.[8]

And so I would pray, "Lord, send in the hornets!"

When my first-born Steve was diagnosed with prostate cancer, there was some question that the cancer had spread into his femur. I had three pages of scripture to reinforce my prayer for his healing. I was amazed at how many verses pertain to the bones. Steve called me from the doctor's office. "Mom, you over-prayed; they can't penetrate my bone because it's so strong!" Bottom line, no cancer in the bones, and he had a robotic surgical procedure to remove the prostate. Every report since then has been zero. He never even missed a Sunday at church!

God is faithful to watch over His word and He hastens to perform it (Jer. 1:12, KJV). I told the Lord once that I thought He did not "hasten" but He was very slow. His reply was, "You think *I'm* slow?"

We miss so much by not being patient, not persevering, quitting too soon, and not waiting on His perfect timing. His ways are higher than our ways, and while many times we may not understand our answer, He promises that one day it will all be clear to us (1 Cor. 13:12), and He is working *all* things "together for good to those who love God, to those who are the called according to His purpose" (Rom. 8:28, NKJV).

A reporter was questioning Mother Teresa about her success. Mother Teresa answered, "God doesn't require us to succeed, he only requires that you try."[9]

We see the importance of having God's Word stored in our hearts. When I received the baptism of the Holy Spirit in 1975, I was given a hunger for the Word. If I could have eaten it to get it inside of me, I would have gladly done it. That desire has not diminished over the years. David says it well in Psalm 119:103: "How sweet are thy words unto my taste! Yea, sweeter than honey to my mouth!" (KJV).

The apostle James talks about the "implanted word," and says that we are to be "doers of the word, and not hearers only" (James 1:21–22, NKJV).

In Acts 14:8–10, Paul encountered a man who had been crippled from birth, and in verse 9, we read that Paul "observed that he had faith to be healed" (NKJV). My question is: how do you see faith? We know Paul had faith because he was teaching, preaching, and healing. He was acting on his faith, but this man? He was crippled, just sitting there. Paul looked at the man; what did he see? Was the man intently listening, squirming, leaning forward, moving his torso back and forth? Paul saw, and then Paul said with a loud voice, "Stand up straight on your feet!" And the man leaped and walked because he believed God's Word and acted on it.

The Word in us is released by our words, and by our actions, and especially in our prayer, which is a combination of words and action. Prayer is a deliberate action of the soul. We are told to "pray without ceasing" and to pray with an attitude of gratitude (1 Thess. 5:17–18). It's just good manners to say "thank you" when you receive.

Before every major decision, Jesus prayed. Many times He went apart by Himself to pray, and then He would choose His disciples, go into this or that place to preach, teach and do miracles, and oh, how He prayed in the Garden of Gethsemane before His crucifixion, so intently that He sweat drops of blood.

The disciples saw the importance of prayer and asked

Him to teach them to pray—not how to raise the dead, heal the sick, cast out demons, feed thousands—but how to pray. That was the essential element they needed to maintain their relationship with God, and the works flowed from there.

God's Word is positive and affirmative! Don't get "hung by the tongue." Keep your confession in line with God's Word, and keep your prayer grounded there.

We can stop the miracle action of God's Word by admitting doubt into our consciousness. Doubt is a thief. Remember the parable of the sower? Satan has no new bag of tricks. In the garden he tempted Eve with, "Did God *really* say?" And she took the bait.

After Jesus was baptized by John the Baptist, the Holy Spirit led Him into the wilderness, where He was tempted by the devil (Luke 4:1–13, NKJV). Satan twists the Word of God. It is a bit ludicrous—Satan trying to tell *the* Word what the Word says. That "S" on Satan's T-shirt must stand for "Stupid!"

In verse 3, he begins, "If you are the Son of God, command this stone be made into bread." Jesus replies, "It is written..."

Moving on, the devil offers Jesus the glory of all the kingdoms of the world, *if* Jesus would worship him. Again Jesus replies with the Word and tells Satan to get behind Him.

Then Satan took Jesus to the pinnacle of the temple in Jerusalem. "If You are the Son of God, throw Yourself down from here...'He shall give His angels charge over you, to keep you.'" The devil is quoting a portion of Psalm 91, but not the whole, just taking one part out of context.

Jesus replies again, "It has been said." Then the devil departs, for a season. One thing you can truthfully say about Satan: he is tenacious, and he wants to plant that seed of doubt in your heart to stop your miracle.

In Matthew 14:27–31, there is the account of Peter walking on the water. You have to admire this brash disciple; he got out of the boat when the others did not. He walked toward Jesus, but then he saw the wind boisterous and fear set in; he began to sink. Peter cried, "Lord, save me!" Immediately Jesus reached forth His hand to catch Peter, and said to him, "O you of little faith, why did you doubt?" (NKJV).

Don't you know Jesus wanted Peter to stand with Him, right there on the water! Sometimes our circumstances appear "boisterous" and we take our eyes off Jesus, The Word. Give doubt an inch and it will take a mile. Doubt and faith cannot co-exist.

In Luke 12:22–30, Jesus said to His disciples, "Therefore, I say to you, do not worry about your life, what you will eat; nor about the body, what you will put on." They are told to consider the ravens and the lilies of the field, how God cares for them, and He asks: "How much more will (God care) for you, O you of little faith?" (NKJV). He admonishes them not to "have an anxious (doubtful) mind" (v. 29).

God is the foundation of our prayer. It is His will that we pray; it brings Him pleasure. The Holy Spirit plants the prayer in our heart, and we speak it forth on earth. The Father is watching over His Word and hastening to perform it. Jesus is our High Priest and Intercessor, and we come in the authority of His Name. He told us to ask in His Name and assures us that we will receive (John 14:13). The Trinity is working here: Father, Son, and Holy Spirit, and we come into agreement with the Three-in-One. This is blessed assurance; we cannot fail!

> Ask, and it shall be given you; seek, and ye shall find; knock, and it shall be opened unto you; for every one that asketh receiveth, and he that seeketh findeth; and to him that knocketh, it shall be opened
>
> —MATTHEW 7:7–8, KJV

Do you see the formula here? A-S-K: Ask, seek, and knock.

That promise He gave you, that prayer in your heart, is watched over until it comes to fruition. God wants you to win, and He will do all in His power to encourage, edify and exhort you. He is a God of integrity, and His Word is His bond.

When my husband Bob left, I went on our deck to pray. The Lord spoke to my heart: "Remember that time on the plane?" I knew He was talking about the time Bob and I departed Atlanta on a flight to California. It was gray and raining, but when we got above the clouds, the sun was shining, turning the clouds into gold. It took my breath away, and I thought to myself, "This must be what the streets of gold in heaven will look like!" I just kept that to myself and would think about it from time to time.

I knew this was God speaking to me because only He would know that special memory. Then He promised that He would be my Son-Light, He would walk with me through this, and when I got to the other side, I would have a good marriage.

I thought I would have a short wait; Bob would come to his senses, ask Jesus into his heart, and come home. But the years began passing by, and many times Satan would whisper, "Did God really say?" Yet every time, I would receive confirmations, signs that I was on the right track. God was watching over me and His Word.

Shortly after Bob left, Susan, a co-worker and friend of mine, went on her lunch hour to a local Christian book store. As she was browsing, a clerk approached and gave her a small block of cedar, on which is a copper butterfly and a tiny blue page of scripture, which says in yellow letters: "God is perfecting that thing that concerneth me" (Ps. 138:8). [I held up the block of cedar, which I have kept all these years.] The clerk said that Susan had a friend who was going through a very hard time, and she was to give this to her. Susan knew it was me. She offered to pay but the clerk declined, saying it was a gift.

When I came home that evening, I had a card of encouragement from a couple in our church, and it quoted the same scripture. Hooray, God is perfecting Bob!

I telephoned my mother with the news, and she said the clerk was an angel. The next day at work I told Susan what my mother had said, so she went back to the store but the clerk was not there. She spoke to the manager, described the clerk and the circumstances, and he said they never had anyone working for them that fit that description. She offered to pay, but the manager refused—it was a gift!

Two years later the divorce was granted, and I was in shock. This was not supposed to happen; Bob was coming home. Often in my times of prayer, words would come into my mind: "No evil shall befall you, nor shall any plague shall come near your dwelling" (Ps. 91:10, nkjv). But I was divorced; that was the plague! The God spoke to my heart: "No, I removed the plague from your dwelling. You're still standing, aren't you?"

One day, as I was turning the pages of my Bible, looking for comfort, I stopped at Isaiah 54. It was just for me, and the words filled my heart: Jesus was my husband, He comforts me when, as a wife of my youth, I had been rejected. And He told of the covenant, the sign of the rainbow, and He would give me sapphires, precious stones (see v. 4–11.) Even my name, "Smith," was in v. 16. At that time my material world was in turmoil: broken down washer, dryer, dishwasher, stove, and hot water heater, rotted bathroom floor, leaking roof, cracked block on my car, and termites! I had to laugh! Lord, have you looked around this place?

On Mother's Day, my children gave me this ring I am wearing today: an opal (rainbow) surrounded by sapphires (precious stones). They had gone to Service Merchandise and knew this was the one. I showed them how I had marked the scripture in my Bible.

My Lord, knowing me, gave me tangible evidence of His promise: my block of wood (like my hard head), and my ring. I began to see also how God was not working just in Bob, but in me! I needed perfecting, maturity.

I had other signs through the years, like birds on telephone wires, more rainbows, and at the base of Vernal Falls in Yosemite, I found *three* angel pennies. Angels drop pennies to remind us to trust in God. He is constantly giving us signs of encouragement because He wants us to persevere. It could be certain scripture that lights up as you read, or lyrics of a song stir your spirit or a word fitly spoken—all just for you because God wants you to be victorious and His Word to prevail.

Abraham's story is familiar to all of us—how God called him to go to another land, and the ups and downs of that calling.

> The word of the Lord came unto Abram in a vision, saying, 'Do not be afraid, Abram. I am your shield, your exceeding great reward.
> —GENESIS 15:1, NKJV

There is a dialogue between God and Abram (later re-named "Abraham," which means "father of many nations"). Abraham is reminding God that he is childless, but God assures him that he will have descendants, so many they could not be numbered.

> And he believed in the Lord, and He accounted
> it to him for righteousness.
> —Verse 6

God continues:
> I am the Lord, who brought you out of Ur of
> the Chaldeans to give you this land to inherit it.
> —Verse 7

And, so like us, Abraham wants a confirmation. In His grace and great patience, God instructs Abraham: "Bring Me a three-year-old heifer, a three-year-old female goat, a three-year-old ram, a turtledove, and a young pigeon. Then he brought all these to Him and cut them in two, down the middle, and placed each piece opposite the other; but he did not cut the birds in two" (vv. 9–10).

God guides and God provides; Abraham follows the instructions. In verse 11, we see a great truth: "And when the vultures came down on the carcasses, Abram drove them away." God didn't drive them away; Abraham did! We learned in the parable of the sower that the birds of prey do come to steal the Word, to rob us of our promises. *We* must drive them away, by standing on the promises of God, wielding the mighty Sword of the Spirit, the Word of God.

There is a hymn I love called "Standing on the Promises."[10] It encapsulates all I have been trying to convey in this teaching today. I wondered how the writer came to the knowledge of this truth, what experiences he had gone through to learn these life lessons, so I did a search on Russell Kelso Carter.[11]

He was born November 18, 1849 in Baltimore, Maryland; he made a personal decision for Christ when he was fifteen in the Presbyterian Church (like me, except I was thirteen); he graduated from Pennsylvania Military Academy in 1867, and became an instructor there two years later. He was commissioned as a captain in the Pennsylvania State Line; he taught chemistry and natural sciences. He developed heart trouble and went to California for three years as a sheep rancher to strengthen his health. He returned to Boston and was healed by a prayer of faith, so he went back to work as a professor of civil engineering and advanced mathematics. By the end of 1879, he was hungry for more of God and received the baptism of the Holy Spirit at a Methodist meeting (like me). He then did some writing (like me), books and hymns, and became an evangelist. Later he developed what he called "brain prostration," (I'm not claiming that one), and after a period of time, received healing at a camp meeting (I love camp meeting). Two years later, he developed malaria but recovered after two weeks. At this time he was going through marital problems, his wife being mentally ill, and they divorced (like me), which was scandalous at that time. He wrote "Standing on the Promises," his most famous hymn, in 1891. After 1891, he had some ups and downs in his faith journey. He remarried, later developed tuberculosis and was healed through prayer and medicine, and interestingly enough, he became a doctor. He was listed as a physician in the 1900 Federal Census, and he continued his work as a doctor until his death in 1928.

We are not hanging in there! Like Dr. Russell Kelso Carter, we are standing on the promises of God—to the glory of the Father, in the strong and mighty name of our Lord Jesus Christ, by the Power of the Holy Spirit!

Now, turn to your neighbor and ask, "How ya doing?"

If they answer, "Standing on the promises," give them a big hug. If they say, "Hanging in there," respond in Christian love and pray for them.

After the folks settled down, Pastor James gave an altar call. Many came forward, and it was especially touching to see husbands and wives coming down together for prayer. I was filled with peace and joy, and a sense of gratitude that I was chosen to re-present Jesus at such time as this. I never felt I was the best choice, but I did answer "Yes" to the call.

Chapter Seven

My Eventful Day

O N May 18, 2010, I was taught a fresh and very personal lesson on intercessory prayer. The interesting aspect was that I was scheduled to speak the following week at a local church on the subject of intercessory prayer. The title of my talk was "The Privilege and Power of Intercessory Prayer." Apparently the Lord wanted me to have a hands-on experience to enforce the teaching; I know for a fact that He does not waste anything!

I was on Camp Creek Parkway proceeding across the intersection at Fulton Industrial Boulevard, both roads being divided highways with turn lanes on each side.

I had a green light and was surprised to see a black van coming at me from the left side. I thought, "He's going to hit me!" and he did! He clipped the rear end of my car and sent me spinning across four lanes of traffic, between two steel poles, into a clump of trees. I was pretty much threading the needle. I did not know what to do, because if I steered to my right, I would hit all the cars stopped on Camp Creek, and if I went to the left, I would go into the traffic on Fulton Industrial, so I was just hanging on for dear life. I was astonished this was happening to me, and I said out loud, "My work isn't finished!" As I saw all the tree branches and leaves coming at me through the windshield, I cried out, "Jesus, Jesus, help me—Jesus, Jesus!" and He did!

My car was on its side; a woman was yelling, "Can you hear me? Are you all right?" I waved my left arm in the air, and said, "No, I'm not all right." Actually, I was dazed and felt like I had gone through a blender. As I looked up and out my side window, I saw four Hispanic men. One of them said, "We can do this," and on the count of four, they lifted my car. The air bag had deployed, knocking off my sun glasses and scraping the right side of my face, but the glasses were neatly folded and laying on the ledge between the window and the door panel. The firemen were right there, along with the paramedics and the police. An officer asked the whereabouts of the other driver, and a witness replied that he had seen everything, and it was not my fault; that the second car had struck me and kept going. The driver had pulled over to the median, looked back, and then drove away.

I was taken to Cobb General Emergency, and after

x-rays, they confirmed that I did not have any broken bones. My daughter came and as we were leaving the hospital, my dear friend Barbara approached us. She had worked as a nurse at Cobb for many years and was now retired. She said that in her devotion time that morning, the Lord told her to pray for me, so she prayed a general prayer, and then finished her reading. The Lord insisted again that she pray for me, and she prayed that He would protect me and keep me safe. She asked the time of the accident, and I replied, "8:30 a.m.," the same time she had been praying.

Another friend from Sunday school, Joan, told me that she awoke at 5:30 a.m., and she had also prayed especially for me.

I had no problem forgiving the hit-and-run driver, as I suspected he had no insurance and needed to avoid serious trouble. It was clear that he had run the light. At the time of the accident, I was on my way to my volunteer job at Family Life Ministries, where we minister to the homeless, the poor, and those in distress. I had been serving there since my retirement as a legal secretary in 1999, so I had seen that side of life - the struggles, discouragement and despair. I prayed for that driver to experience the love of Jesus, as I just did—for the "zillionth" time.

I have some friends who will not drive anymore because of fear. I confess that I had not been sensitive to their viewpoint, until it happened to me. I thought I had all this handled—no bitterness or unforgiveness. Physically, I had some soft tissue and muscle strain, but I was coming out of this. Yet when I got behind the wheel again, fear welled up inside me. I was expecting every car I saw to hit me; that I was a target. Intersections were especially frightening, and I slowly passed through them. When cars would blow their horns, I had to fight back the tears. A big truck tooted at me, and I cried, "Don't do that!" I was like a package with yellow tape cross me, marked "Fragile, Handle with Care."

I have heard all my life that when a horse bucks you off, you have to get right back on. And so I did, with the Lord's help, and each day I had the strength I needed. Paul in the New Testament was also going through a difficult time, "a thorn in the flesh," and he asked the Lord to remove it, but the Lord said: "'My grace is sufficient for you, for My strength is made perfect in weakness.' Then Paul replied: 'Therefore most gladly I will rather boast in my infirmities, that the power of Christ may rest upon me'" (2 Cor. 12:9, NKJV).

So, when we are weak, then we are dynamite!

Since I know God does not waste anything, the question here was not "why," but "what?" What are you trying to teach me, Lord? The obvious is patience and perseverance, but what is this "intercessory prayer?" What makes it so different from just ordinary prayer petitions—like I need favor to get that job, I need a parking place, I need this, I need that, bless Aunt Susie. These are all just fine, but intercession goes deeper. Barbara prayed generally for me, but the Lord required more.

Webster's Dictionary defines intercession as "to mediate, plead on behalf of another." The definitions in *Vine's Expository Dictionary of New Testament Words* are similar, except it goes further to say: "A technical term in approaching a king, and so for approaching God in intercession; seeking the presence and hearing of God on behalf of others."[12]

We see that intercessory prayer is all about others, and Jesus has been called the man for others. The little acronym for "JOY" is: "J" for Jesus, "O" for others, and "Y" for yourself. The master intercessor, of course, is Jesus. His life revolves around others.

> The Lord has sworn and will not relent, You (Jesus) are a priest forever according to the order of Mechizedek...He (Jesus) always lives to make intercession for them (us).
> —HEBREWS 7:21, 25, NKJV

Our Lord Jesus is right now interceding for you and me, at the right hand of the Father, claiming us as His own and validating our prayers. If that doesn't give you a thrill, then "your wood is wet!"

Toward the end of His ministry, Jesus began to explain to the disciples that He would be leaving them soon, and He gave them this promise: "Most assuredly, I say to you, whatever you ask the Father in my name He will give you...Ask, and you will receive, that your joy may be full" (John 16:23–24, NKJV).

Praying in His name means that we come to the

Father on the basis of the completed work of His Son; therefore, we come with confidence.

> Now this is the confidence we have in Him, that if we ask anything according to His will, He hears us. And if we know that He hears us, whatever we ask, we know that we have the petitions that we have asked of Him.
> —1 JOHN 5:14-15, NKJV

It is comforting to know that Jesus prays for us in heaven, but He also prayed for us on earth before He ascended. In His priestly prayer in John 17:20 NKJV: "I do not pray for these alone (the disciples), but also for those who will believe in Me through their word." (That's you and me!)

And Dutch Sheets says, "God chose, from the time of the Creation, to work on the earth through humans, not independent of them. He always has and always will, even at the cost of becoming one. Though God is sovereign and all-powerful, Scripture clearly tells us that He limited Himself, concerning the affairs of earth, to working through human beings."[13]

I heard a story years ago that illustrates this principle: When Jesus ascended into heaven, the angels asked who would be carrying on His work on earth. He answered, "There are these eleven guys." The angels laughed and asked, "What's your alternate plan?" He replied, "There is no alternate plan!"

When Jesus completed His work of atonement on the cross, He cried with a loud voice: "It is finished

(John 19:30, NKJV)." The second Adam won back what the first Adam had lost, enabling His followers to pray from the position of victory, not defeat. The enemy that comes against us in one way, the Lord will cause to flee seven ways; we are "the head and not the tail" (Deut. 28:7, 13).

There is power in united intercessory prayer. In Deuteronomy 32:30, we read that "One (can) chase a thousand and two put ten thousand to flight" (NKJV). Can you see how our power is multiplied? Jesus also promised: "If two of you agree on earth concerning anything that they ask, it will be done for them by My Father in heaven, for where two or three are gathered together in My name, I am there in the midst of them" (Matt. 18:19–20, NKJV).

A dear family in our church transferred to Nashville, Tennessee, but shortly after their move, their teenage daughter, K.J., developed leukemia. They were miles away, but there is no distance in prayer. The family had a web site so we had daily postings and knew what the particular need was at that time and how to pray. We went through the treatment regimen with them, and after two years, K.J. was pronounced cancer free. God used our prayers, not just for K.J. and her family, but all who came in contact with them. Our church saw the power of intercessory prayer, and we grew in faith and unity.

We have all the weapons we need, including the whole armor of God set forth in Ephesians 6:13–17, NKJV: Our waist is girded with truth, we have on the breastplate of righteousness, our feet are shod with the preparation of the gospel of peace, and above all is the shield of faith. The helmet of salvation protects our mind, and we victoriously wield the Sword of the Spirit, which is the Word of God. Verse 18 is vital: "Praying always with all prayer and supplication in the Spirit, being watchful to the end with all perseverance and supplication for all the saints."

It is important to note that all this armor is utilized through prayer for the saints, and it is "watchful" prayer, being the "watchman on the wall" (Ezek. 3:17). That is intercessory prayer!

We are also admonished, before we put on our armor (Eph. 6:10), to "be strong in the Lord and in the power of His might" (NKJV).

Dutch Sheets tells a cute story about a mouse and elephant who were best friends that brings this point home: "They hung out together all the time, the mouse riding on the elephant's back. One day they crossed a wooden bridge, causing it to bow, creak and sway under their combined weight. After they were across, the mouse, impressed over their ability to make such an impact, said to the elephant, 'We sure shook up that bridge, didn't we?'"[14]

We must remember the source of our power; God gets the glory!

There was a particular occasion when I was called to pray *hard* for a friend of mine, who was on a mission to Ecuador. I sensed in my spirit that she was in great distress, and the words "Danger, Danger" kept flashing across my mind. I knelt and prayed fervently for her until the "Danger" passed, and I knew she was safe. When she returned home, I called to hear her report on the trip. She made no mention of any incident, so I asked what had happened on that certain evening, and told her how I was called to intercede. She said she was so ashamed; that she was not going to tell anyone. She got angry with the team leader and left the group to return to the hotel. It is a cardinal rule that you never leave your group! It was very dark, and she was lost. Then she saw a man following her, and she was frightened. Another man approached, asking what she was doing out on the street all alone in that neighborhood at night. She explained she was lost, so he walked with her to the safety of the hotel.

In Matthew 9:38, Jesus tells us to "pray the Lord of the harvest to send out laborers into His harvest" (NKJV), and Paul requests, "Pray for us, that the word of the Lord may run *swiftly* and be glorified" (2 Thess. 3:1, NKJV). We know that all these things are God's will, so why do we have to ask Him for something He already wants to do? Is our asking connected to the releasing of His power? Do we have not because we ask not (James 4:2)?

We know that it is God's will that we pray. For example, He would not forgive Job's "friends" until Job interceded for them (Job 42:8). Jesus gave us the authority to pray in His name (John 16:23), and He watches over His Word and hastens to perform it (Jer. 1:12 KJV). The Holy Spirit takes hold with us against the enemy, helping us when we don't know how to pray (Rom. 8:26). In Old Testament times, the priests would offer sacrifices and intercede for the people, but because Jesus offered Himself, the ultimate sacrifice for sin, His followers are now a royal priesthood (1 Pet. 2:9); we are His intercessors here on earth, dispensing His grace through cracked pots. It's fine to be a cracked pot because more of God's light shines through! It gives new meaning to the chorus we sang as children in Sunday school: "This Little Light of Mine, I'm Going to Let It Shine!"

Witness Lee contends that the Trinity can be compared to electricity. The Father is the source, Jesus is the current, and the Holy Spirit is the transmitter, who sends the power into us.[15]

When we pray, we are not sending words out into the atmosphere, but we are stirring up mighty forces in heaven and on earth: Father, Son, and the Holy Spirit, who dispatches His angels to carry out their assignments. That's why the enemy tries to thwart our prayers—the telephone rings, someone comes to the door, our minds wander, we are suddenly very thirsty, etc. We get off focus.

Get your answer before you pray. In Isaiah 1:18, the Lord says, "Come now, and let us reason together." That means to state your case before the Divine Council (Father, Son, and Holy Spirit); declare the basis for your petition, your prayer. I worked for lawyers for forty-five years, and you can be sure we had our precedents, our evidence, and our facts before going to court.

Dutch Sheets writes: "I believe our prayers do more than just petition the Father. I've become convinced that in some situations they actually release cumulative amounts of God's power until enough has been released to accomplish His will."[16]

When my husband Bob left that certain Sunday afternoon, ending twenty-six years of marriage, I desperately prayed, and the Lord promised restoration. I told a friend that I was interceding for Bob, and she said, "One day that last prayer will push down the wall between him and God." I prayed from 1978 to 2004, and many times it was that travailing prayer (weeping and groaning). One day I felt in my spirit that something was about to happen; I asked the Lord to let me know when it did, and I continued praying. Approximately one week later Bob called me from his home in Mississippi, and during our conversation he accepted Jesus as his Lord and Savior. That final prayer had pushed down the wall! There was restoration between Bob and God, and four years later I received my miracle of restoration. Bob and I agreed we were soul-mates, and I got my happy ending, just like He promised!

The Lord told me once that He has a network over the earth. For example, if He sees a need in my area, He will call on me. You don't have to be there in person, but in the Spirit, as there is no distance in prayer. If you are sensitive to the Holy Spirit, He will use you as His instrument. That is why we must be on "ready." If you miss your call, He will move to someone else.

Remember Esther? She was born "for such a time as this," but Mordecai warned that if she did not answer, God would raise up someone else (Esther 4:14, NKJV). We, too, are born for such a time as this.

I was honored to serve with four other women on a mission trip to China in 2001. Our main goal was to smuggle in Bibles. We each had two suitcases—one for clothes and one for Bibles. We had given our itineraries to prayer partners at home, and we were going through customs in Beijing right on time, 11:00 a.m., which was 11:00 p.m. back home. The plan was to keep spaces between us so if one were stopped, the others might get through. Suddenly Trish, our leader, ran to the last two of us, urging us to come quickly. We ran after her, and as we passed the customs area, the examiner was daydreaming, staring at the wall, so we just ran through the exit. When we returned home, a friend called Trish, asking what happened during customs, as the Lord had awakened her and told her to pray. She prayed the examiner would turn his back to the wall and we would go through unhindered. That prayer partner was serving the Lord through intercessory prayer, just as much as we were in China, smuggling Bibles.

As followers of Christ, we are called to be intercessors, to go into our world and re-present Jesus. It is our privilege and honor, and we have the power.

Just be sure to fasten your seat belt (glad I did)!

You are in for quite a ride!

Chapter Eight

To Italy With Love

TWO OF MY granddaughters, Katy and Abby, graduated from McEachern High School the last of May, 2010, and they were both bound for the University of Georgia that fall. My daughter Stacey, the mother of Abby, is always looking for excuses to travel, and Brenda, my daughter-in-love and mother of Katy, is a more than willing accomplice. They agreed this was a marvelous opportunity to celebrate the dual graduation with a month-long trip to Europe. It would be educational, of course! Steve (my son, Brenda's husband and father of Katy) was easy to persuade; however, it took a bit more time and persuasion for Russell (my son-in-love, Stacey's husband and Abby's father) to get on board.

The plan was that all the girls would leave first,

including Maddie, my other granddaughter (Stacey's daughter), and they would cover England, France, Switzerland, Germany, Austria and the northern part of Italy. Two weeks later, the guys, which included Steve, Russell, and my grandson Matt (Steve's son), and I would depart to meet the girls in Venice, Italy. This was especially appealing to me because I had been to the places the girls were covering first, but not southern Italy. Also, I wanted to get away from automobiles and traffic, as I was still gun-shy, so paddling in boats in Venice just hit my spot! The only hindrance was the pain in my back, side and neck, but, hey, that's what muscle relaxers and extra-strength meds were created for—so we can take a licking and keep on ticking!

Ryan, my remaining grandson, drove us to the airport. I wanted so much for him to go with us, but his job was to get a job, as he had recently graduated from the University of Georgia and it was time for him to launch into the business world. To me, he was still my little first-born grandson, who stood on my coffee table in his white socks, twisting his "be-hind," holding his microphone, and pretending to be Elvis Pressley. I wanted to sneak him into my overnight bag, but we would never have passed security, so I carried him in my heart.

When you are on an airplane, you have a captive audience, and I always pray for opportunities to share my faith, with wisdom. On one side of me was a young man who was traveling to a city north of Venice to attend a seminar, which would give him credit toward a master's degree in business administration. He had experienced a painful divorce, and his heart was still sore.

On the other side of me was a beautiful young lady, very pregnant with a son to be born a few months later. They lived north of Venice so she advised our companion on the best transportation to arrive at his destination. She was excited about being a mother, and the attendant responsibilities.

This is just like the Holy Spirit, to put you in situations where you can relate. I could feel the young man's pain and was able to share how the Lord brings you through the heartache, not wasting a thing. I related also to the young mother's excitement and apprehension. At one time, I was not sure I would ever be a mother—and then I had three children! She was partnering with God in a miracle! I also testified of our Lord's faithfulness to deliver me from the car accident a few weeks earlier; He has plans for us, and they are awesome!

Upon arrival in Venice, the first order of business was to exchange our dollars for Euros. It is amazing to me that you can go to a machine, punch in some numbers, and out comes the currency you need to transact business in that country. I admit that I adapted to this modern miracle, but always with butterflies in my stomach, not wanting to punch the wrong button and wipe out my account. I did come through in the end, unscathed, but with much less wealth than when I left home. But how can you put a dollar value on a trip of memories that can never be duplicated?

We took a water taxi to the city. I had looked forward to the water, but it was raining, so water over and under was a bit much. I am a great fan of Jeopardy, a television quiz show, and I remember one question was: "Robert Benchley, the famous comedian, sent a telegram to a friend saying, 'The city streets are full of water! What shall I do?' Answer: What is Venice!"

We were very close to our reunion, and Steve said he was getting "teary" about seeing Brenda and Katy. When we reached the dock, they were not there, so we started to search for the hotel. As we walked along the streets, I was surprised to see so many steps. There are steps when there is no reason for steps, just for show! It was very difficult for me to pull my suitcase, juggle my umbrella, and carry my overnight bag on my shoulder. My aching body was crying, "Enough already!"

At last, the hotel! But our girls were not there either. We checked in, and then Maddie arrived. The rest of the girls had gone to the boat dock, so Steve and Russell went to find them. It was sweet to see them coming in later, holding hands with their sweethearts.

The guys and I were determined to stay awake until Venice bedtime, so we all went to Piazza San Marco, and toured the Doges' Palace in the Palazzo Ducale. Our guidebook says that the palace "is a masterpiece of Gothic architecture (14th–15th Century) in an unusual subversion of equilibrium, the airily light galleries and arcades appear to support a heavy upper structure. This former seat of political and legal affairs boasts a court-yard and lovely apartments filled with canvases by Old Masters (Tintoretto, Palma the Younger, Veronese) depicting the city's great historical events."[17]

Stacey remarked that it was "impressive and stunning," and I agreed, but my granddaughters had seen enough museums and castles, and they were ready to go home. They were in cultural overload.

Abby remarked that this was a "trip," while a vacation is lying beside a pool, soaking up sunshine, and reading a "beach book." I agree that vacations are very nice, but this was the "trip of a lifetime!" And it was just my first day!

We had a nice dinner that evening, and it was a time of much laughter as the girls shared their adventures with the rest of us. One would bounce off the other, with "Remember when . . ." and another story would unfold. There was the time they were lost in Germany, trying to find the hostel. They mistook a stranger for the man who was to meet them, and a lot was lost in translation! Another time Stacey upset them all by suddenly turning off the Autobahn when she saw a sign with the name of a town and castle she had taught about in her Medieval English class, but it was a very good turn, a lovely surprise. There was the "train" story from the night before, when they shared the compartment with, shall we say, two "unique" men. It was like playing "Can You Top This?" and we were all holding our sides with laughter.

After dinner, the adults went back to the Piazza,

which was lit by old-fashioned lanterns against the backdrop of a starry night. A band was playing on a stage in front of the hotel, and people were dancing, singing and clapping with joy. It would be a wonderful thing if the whole world could be this happy, laughing together as a family. It was like a scene from one of the old musicals, but the good part was that it was real!

After a good night of rest and breakfast outside our hotel in our own little plaza, we returned to Piazza San Marco, where we were approached by a man with an "official" badge. He worked for the city council and there was a special promotion that day only; we would be crazy Americans if we did not take advantage of this opportunity. We were given free coupons, which entitled us to water taxi rides to the glass blowing factory, which charged no admission fee. We questioned him specifically as to whether this was a round trip, and he insisted it was. With a nagging feeling that we were being "had," our family boarded the taxi, which took us through many canals so we could see the city up close and personal.

The glass blowing demonstration displayed the amazing artistry of these craftsmen, from the tiniest replicas of animals to beautiful jewelry and huge chandeliers. Then it was time to return to our hotel, but the entrance to the taxi dock was blocked on our side. We tried to explain to employees standing there that we needed to get to the taxi, but we were told it only brought people in, not out. To return, we would have to go by public taxi. Other tourists had been duped as well. We just had to laugh, because we knew all along there was a "gimmick." Still, it had been an unforgettable excursion, and we made another memory.

As we ate lunch in the city, it started to rain again, but that was no problem, because we were leaving town, via water taxi to the train station—destination Florence! My body was protesting at the demand to pull my suitcase over cobblestones and steps and little bridges in the rain. To sit on a luxurious train and gaze at the countryside for a few hours was a delight. My son Scott said that Florence was his favorite city so I was filled with anticipation.

We stayed in a hotel in the middle of town and it was so noisy. There was traffic at all hours, and the constant sound of breaking glass. Restaurants were all around so perhaps instead of washing the dishes, they were being thrown, either into dumpsters or they were bouncing off walls. It's a mystery!

On this leg of the journey, I roomed with the Smiths. They were a bit more subdued than the girls. What I loved most was the terrace on top of the hotel, where we would go in the evenings, just to sit and talk, enjoying the panoramic view of the city and making our plans for the following day. It was hard to believe it was really me experiencing all this history, beauty, and grandeur. What a gift!

After breakfast at the hotel, we departed for Santa Groce Basilica, one of the finest Gothic churches in Italy. It was founded in 1294 and contains numerous masterpieces of paintings and sculptures, as well as the funeral monuments of Michelangelo, Galileo, Machiavelli, and many others. In the side chapels are paintings and frescoes. After a while, you can scarcely take it all in. It's like looking at a tray of luscious desserts—all of them are yummy and it is hard to choose your favorite.

We found a neat mom-and-pop place for lunch. It was like home cooking, not that we were tired of pasta (but we really were). Full tummies make for happy tourists!

It was time to rendezvous here with the Arnold family, consisting of David, wife Sharliss, and daughter Katherine Jane (K.J.). They had been close friends for years and we loved them dearly. David had named his son Steve after my Steve, and my Steve had named his son (Matthew David) after David. K.J. is our victor over leukemia, and I was inspired and encouraged that if K.J. believed she could withstand the rigors of this trip, certainly I could, too.

The Arnolds were having difficulty finding our hotel, but we guided them via cell phones, and Russell walked up the street to bring them into the fold. The gang was all here! The saying is so true: "The more the merrier!"

Now it was time for what I considered to be the highlight of Florence: The David by Michelangelo, housed at the Galleria dell' Academia. Steve and Matt had gone ahead of the rest of us, going immediately to the statue. Steve said, "Mom, I was moved to tears; it's incredible!"

David, seventeen feet high, stands with his sling draped over one shoulder, holding stones in his opposite hand. There is a garland of olive leaves around his head; he is muscular, young, strong, and very handsome. He is nude, but it is not offensive or pornographic; it is an anointed work of art, and it took my breath away. I walked all around it, and then found a seat along a wall so I could just absorb its beauty.

The condensed history is that the Opera had commissioned Agostino, but for unknown reasons, he abandoned the project. Rossellino followed, but his contract was terminated. The Opera was greatly concerned that this huge block of marble remained neglected for twenty-five years, all the while exposed to the elements in the yard of the cathedral workshop. An inventory reported "a certain figure of marble called David, badly blocked out and supine." Michelangelo convinced the Opera he could finish the work. It took him two years to chisel away everything that was not David.[18]

In the Bible, David is referred to as a man after God's own heart (1 Sam. 13:14, NKJV). As I stood there, I prayed, "Lord, make me a woman after your own heart!"

There was much more to see at the Academia, and we didn't miss a thing. But how in the world could you ever top The David? He was worth the whole trip.

Russell had an eventful encounter that afternoon. At the plaza, Russell thought he saw Reggie Jackson, the famous baseball star. As a young man, Russell aspired to be a baseball major leaguer, so this was special.

When approached, Mr. Jackson confirmed that he was indeed "The" Reggie Jackson of baseball fame. Then he began to reprimand Russell for his tobacco habit, saying that Russell must be about forty; that he was a good looking man, and that he had seen men lose their jaws. He gave Russell his card, with e-mail address and all, asking Russell to contact him when he is free. He promised he would send Russell tickets to any game, anywhere, and ended, "You know I can do it!"

Russell excitedly told the rest of us about his historic meeting. I replied, "God must love you very much to send Reggie Jackson all the way to Italy to tell you this!" I wonder what city Russell is going to choose, and if there might be an extra ticket for his "mother-in-love!"

We ended our glorious day with a late supper. Italians don't get started until at least 8:00 o'clock, and they take their own sweet time; it is an occasion. It was a blessing for us to be together, and especially to see K.J. laughing, feeling well, and so very beautiful. Life is good!

It was our last day in Florence and we had a lot to squeeze into a short space of time. We had passed by the Duomo Cathedral numerous times. My ticket says, "Cupola dei Bunelleschi." We could also see this magnificent building from our hotel terrace. The gang was saying they were going all the way to the top. This seemed impossible to me because the walls of the building go straight up, and then the cupola is curved across the top, like a muffin with a rounded top and red icing. I told them they could wave at me from the crest and I would take their picture.

We literally ran to the cathedral because it was raining. We rushed in, bought tickets and started up the stairs. "Wait a minute," I cried. It was not my plan to ascend "hundreds" of stairs, and then climb a rope ladder sideways at the tippy-top. The very thought made my back and neck go into spasms. But I was trapped, so I started up. At the first landing, I told them I would meet them downstairs, so they proceeded. I tried to go around to the guard station, but the way was blocked, and the guard said I had to go to the second landing before I could descend. "It's only ninety-six steps," he said. Well, that additional ninety-six up was not as hard as the many more than ninety-six going down. All steps were uneven and there was nothing to grasp as I came down. At last I made it, and waited on the first floor for my climbers. A service was being conducted, so I found a seat and listened. Of course, I could not understand a word, but the music was inspiring, and you could feel the presence of the Lord. He is so sweet to tuck in those unexpected blessings when they are so needed.

When the rest of the crew came down, Stacey agreed I had made a wise decision. It had been hard to climb that rope, hand over hand!

It was time for a gelato stop (ice cream). We made several of those every day, which accounted for me gaining six pounds even though I walked miles daily.

Guess you could also attribute that to plenty of pasta. Food was never a problem in Italy; it was an event!

After our break, we proceeded to the Galleria degli Uffizi, where the Caravaggio exhibit was being held. There was art everywhere, even on the ceilings. As you walked, you found yourself "oo-ing" and "ah-ing" and by the end of the tour I was saturated, but in a good way.

It was time to eat again, but all the restaurants were crowded because it was Saturday afternoon. We bought drinks at one place just so we could sit down until the Pizza Parlor could seat us. The pizza was worth the wait! David had a mug of beer that probably held two gallons!

The weather had cleared so we took a long walk to the Arnau River, and climbed more steps for the view of the city at the top. Then it was down, across the covered bridge and back to the shops in town. David took K.J. back to the hotel for a nap and some rest, and Sharliss very kindly slowed her pace and walked with me. This is so typical of that family—caring, compassionate, and considerate.

My son Scott had given me money to spend in Italy; he wanted me to get something special. I chose a leather purse and my other son, Steve, helped me with my purchase. This was another surprise blessing right there in the plaza, knowing both my sons were demonstrating their love for me. Later that day David bought me a bottle of water! God is in the little things!

We ended our day with a picnic supper on the hotel

terrace. We were recalling the events of the day, but then the rains came, forcing us into the dining room. All were agreeable to "early to bed" on our last night in Florence.

The next morning the ladies wished our guys a happy Father's Day and after a last meal at our hotel, we left en masse for the long walk to the station to catch our train for Lucca. I was dragging the rear, as usual, when I noticed that my ring was gone!

This was no ordinary ring, but the one my children gave me in 1980, after the divorce was granted on February 1. I had been searching my Bible for comfort, and when I came to Isaiah. 54, the words spoke to my heart.

I started with verse 4, where the Lord told me to "Fear not," and in verse 5, He promised to be my husband, and in verse 6, He called me as "a wife of youth when (I) was refused. " (I was married at age eighteen.) In verse 9, He spoke of the "waters of Noah" and His promise as evidenced by the rainbow. In verse 10, He said that "the covenant of His peace (would not) be removed," and in verse 11, He spoke of sapphires. Verse 14 said that "In righteousness shalt thou be established," and in verse 16 (KJV), He had my name, "Smith."

It had been hard to remove my wedding ring; I would constantly run my thumb over the place it had been for so many years. After coming home from church on Mother's Day, I was in the kitchen putting the finishing touches on lunch when my children came in, along with Brenda, at that time Steve's future wife.

They had a gift for me and I was overwhelmed. It was an opal ring surrounded by sapphire chips. They had pooled their money and when they went to the store, they knew this was the ring. I showed them in my Bible where I had marked the passage from Isaiah. Of course, this was the ring! The opal is the rainbow stone, and God had promised me sapphires. I told them how I had laughed when I read "sapphires" as I reminded Him of the condition of our house and my finances. This ring was tangible evidence to me of His faithfulness; I could touch it. And now it was gone!

I recalled removing it from my ring finger and putting in on my little finger because it felt tight. It must have slipped off as I slept, so it was probably under my bed or tangled in the bed sheets. We were at the station and there was no time to return to the hotel. I would call once we checked into Lucca, and have them make a search. There was a sick feeling in the pit of my stomach, and while I knew I had to let the ring go and trust my Lord to get it back to me, I could not shake the disappointment. Satan was trying to steal my joy; I was in a battle of the mind.

We boarded the train and settled down for our ride north to Lucca. Upon arrival, the clerk at the hotel in Florence advised that no ring had been turned in by the staff; I was to check again the next day. I searched through my luggage to no avail. Hope was fading, and the following day I received again a negative report. Only the Lord knew the whereabouts of the ring, and He was keeping it to Himself.

Paul taught in Phil. 4:6–7: "Don't fret or worry. Instead of worrying, pray. Let petitions and praises shape your worries into prayers, letting God know your concerns. Before you know it, a sense of God's wholeness, everything coming together for good, will come and settle you down. It's wonderful what happens when Christ Jesus displaces worry at the center of your life" (THE MESSAGE).

My Lord had never failed me, and He never would. I offered the ring to Him as a sacrifice of praise. I regret that I had to do this many times, but it finally stuck. The ring was no longer my concern.

Lucca was delightful. Our hotel brochure described the ancient, medieval city that was once a Roman colony in 180 B.C. The Renaissance-era walls surrounding the old city are still intact and wide enough for people to promenade for walking or jogging.

Our hotel was across the street from an entrance to the wall. The girls rented bikes and were pretty much on their own the whole time we were in Lucca. It was an especially poignant moment for K.J. because it was the first time she had ridden a bike since her illness. She loved the independence and her eyes danced with excitement. It was hard for me not to cry for joy.

The rest of our group took a walk through the old city. It reminded me of Jerusalem, the old city surrounded by walls, but in Jerusalem it is stone and rock and not dirt and vegetation. In Lucca, trees lined the walls and there were flowers and grass, a peaceful atmosphere. Old Jerusalem hustles and bustles. Each city has its own flavor.

We visited the Church of San Giorgio and the Bell Tower. It was a 225-step hike to the top, so I waited at the bottom and people-watched. Very interesting! People from many cultures were visiting Lucca that day.

The girls met us for lunch at Girovita. Stacey had a guide book and when we would question her about her choices for dining, her reply would be, "It's in the book!" We made friends with a waitress named Betsy. It is so important to build friendship bridges because it opens doors to witness the love of Christ, and it is good public relations for America. You never know, but you could meet that person again.

There was a flea market in the plaza and we enjoyed the local crafts. We visited the Duomo di San Martino (Cathedral of St. Martin). There are just not enough adjectives to describe the artistry and grandeur of these churches. There is a quiet splendor in each of them, so you must be silent; yet I wanted to praise the Lord and clap my hands in adoration. He is so worthy!

We had to make a gelato stop in the Piazza Anfiteatro. There were shops lining the Piazza and Matt bought a flag of Italy. They were contending in the World Cup Soccer games, so we had become ardent fans.

That evening we went to supper at the Bei & Nannini Caffe and were pleasantly surprised when our waitress was our friend Betsy, from lunch. She came to Italy from Romania and was raised by her grand-mother, whom she considered to be her mother. She thought of her real mother as more like a sister, and we were delighted when she said her own mother was the cook there, and she introduced us to her. Of course, we had to seize this photo-moment! Betsy told us that she planned to be in Vernazza, our next stop, for a little vacation at the beach. We promised to be on the look-out for her, and hoped we would meet again. Our meal was superb, laced with lots of laughter, and there were hugs when we left, loaded with wine, pizza, bread, and sandwiches. I love these little God-surprises!

After breakfast at the hotel, we had just enough time for a short walk along the wall before another quick walk to the train station. We inadvertently took the express train to Vernazza, and the conductor requested we depart. Between train rides, we sneaked in lunch at McDonald's and I had a "Happy Meal," just a little reminder of home. During the last leg of the journey, we were mostly in tunnels, but occasionally we would emerge and catch glimpses of the Mediterranean Sea.

Vernazza is one of five cities comprising the Cinque Terre, meaning "The Five Lands." The cities, which include Monterosso al Mare, Corniglia, Manarola and Riomaggiore, the coastline, and the surrounding hill-sides are all part of the Cinque Terre National Park and is a UNESCO World Heritage Site. Thus far on the trip we had been exposed to cultural beauty (art masterpieces, sculpture, architecture and the like), but this was beauty unsurpassed, created by the Master Himself. It was heavenly!

"The Cinque Terre is noted for its beauty. Over

centuries, people have carefully built terraces on the rugged steep landscape right up to the cliffs that over-look the sea. Part of its charm is the lack of visible "modern" development. Paths, trains and boats con-nect the villages, and cars cannot reach it from the outside."[19]

Stacey, Russell, the girls, Matt, and I stayed in an apartment on the lower side of the hill, which was really a mountain, if you ask me. Sharliss and David were farther up, and Brenda and Steve closer to the top. Abby, Maddie, and I made for the beach while others tended to their chores. Matt was again my roommate. Bless his heart!

The plan was to have supper that night on the tippy-top, many steps above Steve and Brenda. My side and neck were hurting big time, and I begged to stay home; however, my family refused to take "no" for an answer, and all the "young-uns" escorted me up the many, many steps to the top, encouraging me along the way. I was pleasantly surprised that it was not so difficult after all. Matt reminded me, "You made it at Vernal Falls, Yosemite, the mountains, and the water!"

"Yes," I replied. "But I was younger, and didn't have bruised muscles; I had not just totaled my car with me in it!"

There was a glorious view at the top, and I sat at the end of the table with my escorts. It was fun to hear them talking about their plans for the future, including how many children they would have, what they would look like, and even the décor of their homes. Katy was insistent that the family Christmas would be at her house—a tradition. I look forward to that!

My escorts made sure I arrived home safely, and then everyone spread out to do his/her thing. Abby went down the hill to use the internet, the other girls were taking showers, Matt wanted to see the night lights of the city, the adults were undoubtedly at the Arnold's, and my body was crying, "Rest!"

We discovered a yummy place to eat breakfast, just up the street from our place. It was called Il Pirata Delle and run by twin brothers. I'm not sure whether it was in the book or not, but it should be. The brothers were charming, and the food was delicious-o. We made reservations for dinner that night at 7:00 p.m.

The "strong" members of our group decided to hike to the next town. There is a walking trail known as Sentiero Azzurro ("Light Blue Trail") that connects the five villages. The trail from Vernazza to Monterosso, the next village, winds through olive orchards and vineyards, and while it is rough in many places, it offers the best view of the bay. The "weaker" of our clan included Russell and Sharliss because of their knees, K.J. because she was still on her road to total recovery and me, because of the accident and because "My Mom didn't raise no dummies!"

Russell got his ladies to the train station, and we carried all the bathing suits and beach gear. It was a short ride to Monterosso, and after we settled on the beach, we kept a watch for Betsy, but never saw her again. Sometime later, our "Amazons" joined us, extolling their adventure. My adventure suited me fine, stretched out in a beach chair, watching the tide come in, surrounded by brightly colored umbrellas!

I thought about Bob while sitting there. We never took vacations together to Europe, or cruises to South America, but we did take the kids to Daytona Beach and Panama City (what we could afford), and he and I did go to Kansas when he was drafted. Then our paths divided. I went "Around the World in Seventy Years" with "Nothing Wasted," while he also went around the world and on cruises with his "friends." Funny how life happens!

We stayed most of the day and probably would have stayed until dark, but we had dinner reservations, and there was a train to catch—no hiking back.

We did experience another "lost" episode. K.J.'s charm bracelet was missing. We moved chairs, sifted through the sand, and searched all the beach bags, to no avail. I knew exactly how she felt, and was so happy when they found it in David's luggage back at the apartment. She never brought it to the beach. Even when what we believe is incorrect, it still is our reality.

It was good that we had made reservations for supper because the Brothers' place was crowded. The food was awesome and we were having a marvelous time, but many were waiting; we helped clean the tables so they would not lose any business. Keep building those friendship bridges!

It was time to retire for the evening, our last night

in Vernazza, and there was packing to be done. It had been such a glorious day, another gift from God.

There was no time the next morning to do any more sight-seeing. I walked up to the Brothers for breakfast—pastry and hot tea, and they would not let me pay! I wish I could have taken them home with me, but that would be too much of a loss for Vernazza! Goodbye, dear friends.

I walked down to the bay, where the fishermen had just come in with their catch. Stacey, Russell, Steve, and Brenda came shortly after I did, so we seized a few more Kodak moments. My cup was running over! Just wished my son Scott were there to make my family complete.

We took the train to La Spezia, where we transferred to Rome. Steve and Brenda insisted I sit with them, and I did for awhile, enjoying the sharing. Then I moved to the front, where there was more room and I had a big window view. There are times when a gal just needs a little down time!

Rome is a bustling metropolis, exactly the opposite of our lazy, laid back Vernazza. I would have been content to get on a return train and spend the rest of our time in Cinque Terre; however, Rome is the Eternal City and there is much to see. I did not want to miss anything. Also, I had an assignment from the Lord. I was to go to the Vatican and pray for His church, the big "C" (Catholic) and little "c" (universal). Does that sound prideful? I didn't say it out loud to anyone, and I knew that thousands prayed in the Vatican, yet I must be obedient to my call. Perhaps the Lord has a cup of prayer and He needed my drop. I would not withhold it.

There was confusion in contacting our agent in Rome, as we did not have an address, only a telephone number. After waiting almost an hour on a street corner, to the consternation of our young travelers, Julio came to our rescue. He led us to our second floor apartment, which included a living room with a studio couch and bed, kitchen, three bedrooms, and one bathroom, to be shared by the twelve of us. Very interesting! The mustard colored walls were a bit striking. The best thing was that we were two blocks from the Vatican, and we could see it from our bedroom windows. Another big plus was the gelato shop, right at the entrance to our building.

We arrived on Brenda's birthday, and decided to celebrate with dinner at Manichetta, recommended by Julio. We ate outside and were serenaded by a man playing an accordion. He let Abby attempt to play, and when she finally struck a chord, she exclaimed, "I'm so happy!" This was one of the goals in her life; she has a list of 100. Russell bought Brenda a rose, and also one for Stacey. When Steve prayed before our meal, he especially thanked the Lord for Brenda and for our trip. We were all just soaking up the joy.

I slept very soundly, but the girls said I snored. I had never been accused of that before and was embarrassed. My darling Katy tried to soothe my feelings, and said my snoring was very cute. I don't think Abby agreed, as her bed was next to mine and she was the most disturbed. I vowed to myself that I would sleep on my side for the rest of the trip. They were a big help to me and I did not want to lose their favor.

We traveled by subway to the Coliseum. David and Sharliss had been here before so they knew the first order of business was to find a tour guide. You would never understand all the ramifications without an expert, and we were blessed to find Guida. I knew that Christians were fed to the lions here, but was shocked to learn that people who were sentenced to death, gladiators, and even animals, such as zebras and even tiny squirrels—anything to make a show—were put to death to please the Roman citizenry. They were a blood-thirsty group, and violence thrilled them; even the women delighted in the mayhem. The entire scene made me sad—man's inhumanity to man, which is still being played out in our society today.

The Lord's judgment came with a major earthquake in 443. The games eventually stopped when the Emperor became a Christian. Guida said that at one point Jews who had been carried to Rome after A.D. 70 melted down the bronze and metal in the buildings, causing them to collapse, just as the Roman Empire collapsed.

We crossed over the street to the Palatine Hill, and then walked a short distance to the Coelian Hill, which overlooked historic sites, including a large stone arc which the conquered would march through as the Romans paraded them into the city. How sad that all that was left of this great and powerful kingdom were the rocks.

Our guide at this time was Jill, who was originally from Atlanta, home to us, and was getting her doctorate in theology at the Vatican. It really is a small world! She pointed out that we were walking on the very stones on which Peter and Paul had walked. I knew from my trips to Israel that the Bible comes alive there, but I felt the same here in Rome. This was headquarters of the army that occupied Israel; orders came from here, and this is where the head attempted to rule the tail.

We left these significant archaeological treasures for the more light-hearted and beautiful Trevi Fountain. Of course, I had seen the fountain in many movies, but I was elated to be here in person. It was crowded, and it was so nice to see families having fun playing in the water, taking pictures, and making memories. There are bleachers in a semi-circle around the front of the fountain, so it was a good place to rest the body while lifting your spirit.

Our next stop was the Pantheon, which was built in A.D. 118 and is the world's largest dome monument of wood covered in concrete. Here we saw the tomb of Raphael, and had a gelato snack on the front steps—past meeting the future!

We walked past the Castel de Angelo, originally a fortress and a prison in the Middle Ages. There are statues of ten white marble angels lining the bridge to the entrance, each one carrying an instrument of the martyrdom of Christ. There was no time to stop here, much to my chagrin. We just could not pack everything into one day.

When I say we "walked" needs qualification. To be exact, my group was doing a fast trot. My goal was to see everything along the way, look at the people, and remain cautious of the uneven stones and pavement. Their goal was to get to the next destination, post haste. After all, time is flying!

When we reached our apartment, it was crash time. K.J. took a three-hour nap. The "grown-ups" wanted to go out for dinner, and I happily agreed (very happily) to "baby-sit." Steve brought us three pizzas so we had a feast. Later the kids, with the exception of Maddie, went to the internet café, and this gave me some down time with just her. She was a bit nervous about going into her junior year, and it was just good time sharing between G'Ma Bet and Maddie Lou. She is a treasure! The only sad note of the evening was that Italy lost their World Cup soccer round.

We awoke to a beautiful, sun-shiny day, and I was so excited. We were going to the Vatican, and I would carry out my assignment. But first, there was sing-along in the living room with Steve; he carries his guitar everywhere he goes. Then we left for the Metro, but there was the customary strike, so we traveled by bus to the Parco della Villa Borghese. We were in a huge plaza, with the usual beautiful fountain in the middle, looking everywhere for signs to the Gardens. There was a massive flight of steps and people were at the top admiring the view and waving to the people below. Our young ones decided to climb the stairs, and then, of course, the Gardens were at the top! There had to be someone who designed the layout of this city who got a commission for all the steps! He made a bundle here! But it was worth the climb to see the lovely park and flowers, the water clock, the lake and the ducks. Lunch was extra-tasty, as we bought sandwiches from a trolley car and sat on benches, enjoying the scenery.

One funny memory here is going to the ladies restroom, where there was a line waiting, but when I approached, the attendant motioned me to come forward. I declined because others were ahead of me, but she was insistent, grabbing my arm and pushing me inside. I surmised that either I looked very old and tired, or I reminded her of her mother, or the Lord just wanted to bless me. Whatever—I gratefully received the favor!

And now to the "cream of the crop," the "Piece De La Resistance," the Vatican. The line to enter was mega, and I thought we would be there for hours; to my surprise, we moved rather quickly. We were separated, because the guys left to get tickets for the Vatican Museum and Sistine Chapel. Later the Arnolds came for K.J. to rush to the Chapel because this was their last day. I entered the Vatican with my three granddaughters. We were awestruck by the beauty, opulence, and majesty. It is a massive building, filled with sculpture, carvings, and paintings. We saw St. Peter's tomb, along with many others. The main area where mass is held is ornate; I was impressed with the wealth of the Catholic Church.

The girls waited for me as I entered a chapel located off to the side of the main walking area. It was lovely and serene, and I tried to quiet my spirit, as my main goal here was to pray for the Catholic Church and the universal church. It was a simple prayer from my heart, and I regretted I was being pressured because my girls were waiting; I did so much want to spend time here in meditation. The Lord doesn't need a lot of words, and I know I have a tendency to be long-winded. I had to be like Susanna Wesley. When she would pull her apron over her face to pray, the children knew to leave her alone. She would finish praying, take down the apron, and get on with her business. I had carried out my assignment, my girls were waiting, and time was flying!

We met the rest of our group outside. It was neat to see the chimney on the roof of the Vatican, where the color of the smoke indicates the election of a new pope. If it is white, a new pope has been elected; if it is black, no decision has been made.

We walked the short distance to our apartment for a little rest, and then a nice dinner. We topped our extraordinary day with another visit to the Vatican at night. The lights gave it a golden glow, and the moon was shining as a backdrop. Breathtaking!

The Arnolds left early in the morning, a signal that our trip was coming to an end. After breakfast, we walked to the Vatican Museum and Sistine Chapel. The guard was claiming that our tickets were not valid, as they had been purchased the previous day. We explained that we intended to come after touring the Vatican, but we could not make their closing time. We begged for mercy, as this was our last day. He called for a higher authority, and this generous officer gave us a special stamp to enter. Favor is an awesome thing, and we knew Who the Higher Authority really was!

The museum was mind-boggling! There was a hall covered with massive tapestries on each side, and there were even some modern paintings, which seemed so out of place in comparison to the Old Masters. The staircases had railings with intricate carvings. Out one window, we saw the Swiss guards marching, dressed in their colorful, unique uniforms.

Michelangelo's famous Sistine ceiling depicts scenes from Genesis in dramatic moving detail, while The Last Judgment on the end wall is striking and powerful. As if that were not enough, the side walls are covered with impressive Renaissance frescoes by other artists, depicting biblical scenes and contemporary popes.[20]

It took Michelangelo four years (1508–12) to complete the work. I did pick out the famous scene of God's finger touching the finger of Adam.

It was uncomfortable for me to keep gazing at the ceiling as it caused my neck to rebel. How very challenging it must have been for Michelangelo! The chapel was crowded with people who did not want to move to let others inside. The guard would yell for silence, which lasted a short time, and then the volume would get louder, as if someone were turning up their radio, so the guard would yell again, and thus it went, on and on. I would not like to have his job!

When we left, we discovered Matt was missing, so Steve went to find him. The rest of us decided we would spend our time eating lunch at a sidewalk café, so we would catch them as they came by. At every place we ate on the trip, someone would order tiramisu and judge its quality. It was decided that this was the best so far!

After a brief rest and regrouping at our apartment, we rode the bus to the Jewish ghetto area. I had a seat at the front of the bus, and when Stacey saw our street, she yelled, "Get off the bus!" They made it, but I did not, so I rode down to the next stop. I was walking back, and met my grandchildren coming after me.

We passed the Circus Maximus, where the Romans held games. Now it is just a big dirt field with grassy banks. Apparently concerts and flea markets are the main attractions today. From there we ascended a steep hill for a sweeping view of the city from a lovely park filled with orange trees. The fruit covered the ground, and the air was filled with the smell of pungent oranges. This was a grand photo opportunity, as Rome laid at our feet.

As we descended, we passed an old church (everything is old in Rome), where a wedding was being held. The guests were magnificently dressed, and there were expensive sports cars and limousines. Wish we could have seen the bride! We just got a taste.

We came to another plaza, with the traditional

fountain and steps, where people were enjoying a small band playing the xylophone, guitar, and bass. We are a family of musicians (except for me, as I am simply the producer of musicians) so this was great fun for us. Across from us was the Church of Anna Marie, so I excused myself to take a peek. This was another one of God's surprises! The interior of this rather gray drab church was breathtaking. The altar area appeared to be gold, and it shined in the candle light. The congregation was singing, and I wanted to sing with them. I knew the melody, but not the language; still my heart was in tune. I was standing at the rear and Russell walked in, so I knew we had to join the others. One of these days, time will not be an issue!

It began to rain, so we tried to take cover under a leaky awning to wait for Russell to find a restaurant so we could eat supper and wait out the rain. We were concerned because he was gone such a long time. He had fallen on the wet stones and became disoriented, so had trouble finding his way back to us. He is a firefighter, always in control, and never loses direction, so this was most disconcerting and a blow to his pride.

We decided to go into a sports bar for some snacks and to watch the World Cup soccer game. We could dry out a bit and let Russell catch his breath. The rain let up just a bit, so we headed to the bus stop. Sad to say, we departed the bus too soon, and had a very long walk back to our apartment. But in every storm, you can find a rainbow, and we walked up the avenue of angels approaching the Castel de Angelo that I had wanted to see earlier but could not because of time constraints. Thank You, Jesus!

The sun was beginning to set and we saw lovely scenes along the way, such as the view from the river and the wide avenue leading to the Vatican. The sun was immediately behind the Vatican, leaving it in a gray shadow with the soft golden pink behind its back. It was a lovely closing scene.

The rain fell harder and we were running to get home. Sweet Russell and Stacey kept pace with me and we were dripping wet. We were almost there when Steve came running to me with an umbrella. I had to laugh because I could not be anymore wet unless I was under water. Still, it's the thought that counts. When we reached the lobby, we were hysterical with laughter. Steve said that one day we would look back on this and laugh. I replied, "We're laughing *now!*"

Isn't it funny that when you are wet and cold, you want to take a hot shower? We all did, and the braver ones wanted to go out again for dinner (it had stopped raining). Steve, Matt, and I opted out because we just wanted to rest and watch the U.S.A. play in the World Cup soccer. My body was crying, "Give me a break!" Sweet Brenda brought us some pizza. The Lord blessed us when He chose Brenda for Steve; she has a servant's heart, and sees to it that her family's needs are met (Proverbs 31 woman). We watched our country lose to Ghana. It didn't really matter, as we had an unforgettable last day in Rome.

We rode the next morning in taxis to the airport. I was with my granddaughters, and, of course, any taxi ride in a foreign country is an adventure. Your life is literally in their hands. Abby took my carry-on bag as we were going through security, and I heard her excitedly tell the examiner, "It's not my bag! It's my grandmother's!" I had forgotten to remove a water bottle. Ooops! She may love me, but she wasn't going to take the rap for me.

On the plane I was seated next to a very attractive young lady, who had beautiful teeth, so I could relate to her calling to go to medical school and become a dentist. She was active in her Presbyterian Church back in Mobile, Alabama, and she was most attentive to me, showing me how to work the TV remote. One movie I watched was "When in Rome," and it was a delight to see the places I had been. Another sweet surprise!

There was another incident as I passed through security in Atlanta. This time I had forgotten to remove my money belt. Steve was taken to a special area for questioning because of his name, Steven Smith. It is a common name and on the "list," so this was not a new thing for him. At last we exited the airport, and were met by Ryan (my other grandson) and our friend Piper. There is no place like home!

The next morning at home, I awoke very early, as my body was still on Italy time. I asked the Lord what lesson He was teaching me regarding the loss of my ring. I could feel Him say that the precious stones are symbolic of His covenant; that His covenant is in my heart, and the precious stones are alive—they are my family!

Then I prayed that whoever had my ring would be blessed, but I just had to add: "Lord Jesus, You said I could ask anything and You would do it for me. Please give me back my ring."

Later that morning, I unpacked my suitcase, and as I took out the last of my clothes, there in the corner was my ring, plus a dime and two pennies! I know that pennies are dropped by angels as a sign to trust in God, and I had two—a double portion. But what was the dime? I call that Extravagant Love! I wept, thanking Him over and over and over again as He had once more gone "beyond!"

Chapter Nine

Camp Meeting Time
at Indian Springs

THERE WAS A brief turnaround from our arrival
at home from Italy to the beginning of Camp
Meeting at Indian Springs. Reverend Grandfather
Jones built our cottage in 1904, and the family has faithfully attended every year. Grandfather had one son and
four daughters, one of whom was Emma Jones. She
married Ernest Smith, my husband Bob's grandfather.
Accordingly, I married into the Smith-Jones clan, and
have been attending camp meeting since 1950. I am
blessed to be Leaseholder for the family, which means
they give me money at the Family Reunion business
meeting on the first Sunday of the ten-day camp, and
I administer the funds during the year. We are a team,
and have uniquely talented family members. I believe

we have the prettiest place on the grounds; however, I know that "beauty is in the eye of the beholder," and confess that I am prejudiced.

Camp Meeting would be diametrically opposite of our Italian trip, as Camp Meeting means Bible study in the morning, followed by three worship services during the day, with breaks for lunch and supper. The youth and adult have separate tabernacles, both having tin roofs, which make a racket when the rains come, so the speaker is drowned out. The music is incredible. The adult song leader can just start with "Ah" and the congregation follows with "Ah-mazing Grace!" The adults can hear the youth singing, as they start about thirty minutes earlier, and it is not uncommon for the adults to crash the youth services, as they are so dynamic. In the afternoons, the youth have recreation time, which includes the rope glide, swimming, volleyball, and other competitive games, and for the "tweens" it is four square and the "multimegagiga" games. We always have a lot of company to sit on the porch, rock in the rocking chairs, and drink iced tea. We love to share our meals (God always multiplies), and some years we have the missionaries come to eat with us and tell us of their exploits. It's fun to see our kids so excited, asking questions, and making friends with the missionary kids. Our refrigerators at home are covered in missionary pictures, some of whom we help support financially, but always covering them in prayer.

The first Sunday is family reunion, and you can imagine bringing the Jones and the Smiths and their extended families together. We fill the tables in our basement area. "Basement" is actually a dirt floor covered for the most part by outdoor carpeting. The walls on the three sides, which are not directly under the cabin's front porch, are wood about halfway up, and the rest is lattice and screens. In the old days, the floors were covered in sawdust, but that was a smorgasbord for termites. We have slowly moved into the twenty-first century by adding some air conditioning units, a shower, and even a microwave; however, there is no rush. It's just nice to sit in the rockers on the front porch and drink our iced tea.

I was still having pain in my back and neck, and occasionally I would have to lie down awhile, but there were many busy and willing hands. There was a healing service on Saturday morning, and I went forward for prayer. The sweet pastor who prayed for me asked that I not only be physically healed, but that God would take away the inner pain and heal the memories. That was truly what I needed! Not only was my neck and back hurting, but my "feelings" were aching and tender. Driving was nerve racking, and it took courage for me to pass through intersections, as I expected another car to impale me before I could pass safely across. I knew the Holy Spirit had revealed this to my brother-in-Christ; therefore, God would answer this prayer.

Most of the family had come and gone, and from Sunday evening until the following Friday evening, it was the "girls" and Josh, Abby's boyfriend. He was a joy, helping with the heavy-duty stuff; it's just good to have a man around! We had great table conversations, discussing what we had learned at the previous sessions. I was sad to say goodbye to the group Friday evening, but I would see them at home on Sunday evening. I used that Saturday to wash the linens and prepare the cottage for closing.

I was surprised when I awoke Sunday morning to absolutely *no* pain in my back! I twisted and turned every which way; it was *gone*! I started crying for happiness; God had answered that healing prayer! I stilled myself and thanked Him. I heard Him say in my heart that He was healing me in increments—my side, the smaller place in my back, and then the lower back with the severe pain, and last to go would be the neck!

I believe the neck pain is a test. Will I keep praising and serving Him even when I have pain in my neck? Yes, Lord; emphatically I say, *yes*! I know He never stops loving me, even when I am a pain in His neck. I am on my way "beyond!"

Chapter Ten

The Most
Profound Question(s)

A T THE LAST service I attended at Camp Meeting, the evangelist used as his text Matthew 27:15–22 (NKJV), wherein Jesus traded places with Barabbas: "Now at the feast the governor was accustomed to releasing to the multitude one prisoner whom they wished. And at that time they had a notorious prisoner called Barabbas. Therefore, when they had gathered together, Pilate said to them, 'Whom do you want me to release to you? Barabbas or Jesus who is called Christ?' For he knew that they had handed Him over because of envy. While he was sitting on the judgment seat, his wife sent to him, saying, 'Have nothing to do with that just Man, for I have suffered many things today in a dream because of Him.'"

Like a lot of men, Pilate did not listen to his wife. He was under tremendous pressure from the Jewish leaders, and he wanted peace at any price in order to save his own hide. How sad that he sacrificed the Prince of Peace for a worldly peace that still eluded him. Yet, this was a part of the Father's plan.

Continuing in verses 20–22: "But the chief priests and elders persuaded the multitudes that they should ask for Barabbas and destroy Jesus." Note that they did not want just to lay a few stripes on Jesus, they wanted Him *dead*! "The governor answered and said to them, 'Which of the two do you want me to release to you?' They said, 'Barabbas!'"

Think about this: Barabbas has been down in the dungeon, awaiting crucifixion. He can hear all the shouting above him, and he hears his name; the crowd is yelling, "Barabbas! Barabbas!" He is unable to hear the words of Pilate, but only the crowd yelling, "Crucify him, crucify him." Then the soldiers march to his cell, and unlock the door. This is it! But instead of marching him to his death, they tell him that he is free. "*Jesus* is taking your place!" Isn't that what Jesus did for us? When we deserved punishment, death and hell, He died for us; He took our place!

And now Pilate asks the most profound and important question of all mankind: "*What then shall I do with Jesus who is called the Christ?*"

Our answer determines what He will do with us. If we answer correctly, we have eternal life; if we are wrong, we have eternal death. Not to make a choice is to make a choice. Either we crown Him Lord, or we crucify Him.

It is interesting to note the outcome of the choice of rejection that Pilate made, as well as Judas Iscariot, and the wicked King Herod. Both Pilate and Judas committed suicide, and Herod's insides were eaten with worms (Acts 12:23; Matt. 27:5).

Now let's go to John, chapter 20, which contains another profound question, and it is asked by Jesus Himself. This is the account of that first resurrection morning.

Mary Magdalene came to the tomb early, while it was still dark. It was not just dark outside, but dark inside. Jesus had cast seven demons from her, set her free (Luke 8:2), and she loved Him, but He had been crucified. Her world was indeed dark.

When she arrived at the tomb, she was shocked to see that the stone had been rolled away, so she ran to get Simon Peter and John. "They have taken away the Lord out of the tomb, and we do not know where they have laid Him" (v. 2).

John outran Peter, and he looked in, but did not go inside. Brash Peter did go in, and he saw the linen cloths lying there, and the handkerchief that had been around Jesus' head, not lying with the linen cloths but off by itself (vv. 3–8).

Here is a clue: the body of Jesus had been taken by Joseph of Arimathea and Nicodemus, and they had wrapped His body in linen cloths (John 19:38–41). It was also the custom of the Jews to place a handkerchief over the face, and spices would be poured over the face and the body. Isn't it most interesting that the cloths were lying there, like an empty cocoon, but there was no body, and the handkerchief was neatly folded in a place by itself, a deliberate act? Jesus had left evidence of His resurrection.

It is also a Jewish custom that when the master leaves the table where he is eating, he crumples his napkin and places it on the plate, indicating he is not coming back. If he intends to return, he folds the napkin and puts it on the table, so the servant will know not to remove his plate. Jesus folded the napkin, because He is coming back!

Then John went in, "And he saw and believed. For as yet they did not know the Scripture, that He must rise again from the dead" (v. 8–9). John believed from the evidence that Jesus had risen, but he did not fully comprehend all the ramifications. Then the guys went home, but not Mary (v. 11). Don't you love her tenacity, her perseverance? Because of her "stick-ability," she received further evidence—an awesome revelation.

Looking into the tomb, she saw two angels in white sitting, one at the head and the other at the feet, where the body of Jesus had lain (v. 12). This is a picture of the ark of the covenant and the mercy seat (Exod. 37:1–9). The mercy seat would be the slab on which the body of Christ had lain, with an angel at the head and an angel at the foot. This was a New Testament fulfillment of the Old Testament instructions given to Moses. The ark was still in the holiest of holies in the temple, where only the high priest could enter, but Jesus tore open the veil, from top to bottom, making it accessible to all (Luke 23:45), just like the open door to the empty tomb. The stone was not rolled away to let Jesus out, but to let the people in.

The angels ask Mary why she is weeping, and she repeats, "Because they have taken away my Lord, and I do not know where they have laid Him" (v. 13).

Then she turned around and there was Jesus, but she did not know that it was really Him. After all, she thought He was dead and His body had been stolen; she was not expecting to find Him alive (v. 14).

And here we have another profound, most important question, and it is asked by Jesus Himself (v. 15): "*Who are you looking for?*"

Note that He did not ask *what* are you looking for, but *who*! Life is all about a real live person, God-with-skin-on: Jesus! It's about relationship with Him, so that we have access to the Father. Our Elder Brother makes it possible for us to be adopted into the family of God, and to be filled with the Holy Spirit so that we have the power to walk in victory on this earth. Jesus is The Way, our way, our ticket to an eternity that defies our imagination. He is not a *what*, but a *who*!

Then our Lord did a precious thing—He called her by name: Mary. She knew it was Jesus! Don't you know she was trying to hug Him tight, and never let Him go? Then Jesus said to her: "Do not cling to Me, for I have not yet ascended to My Father; but go to My brethren and say to them, 'I am ascending to My Father and your Father, and to My God and your God'" (v. 17).

Jesus had descended into hell to preach to those in captivity, and to set the prisoners free (Eph. 4:8–10). He, as the "first fruit," was taking them home (Col. 1:18). As our High Priest, His blood had to be sprinkled on the mercy seat in the heavenly tabernacle as atonement for our sin (Heb. 8:11–12). Yet He put His mission on hold because Mary was looking for Him. (Can you see Him holding up His hand to Abraham, Isaac, Jacob, Moses, John the Baptist, Ruth, Esther, and all the gang, telling them to wait just a minute, because "Mary" needs Him?) He had to come to her because she mattered to Him! (And so do we!) She was the first to meet the resurrected Christ, and as such, she had the honor of being His missionary to the disciples. She later became a prominent leader in the Christian movement. Talk about going "beyond!"

When my husband left, I was shaken to the core. At my lowest point, I asked myself, "What do I believe that cannot be shaken?" I found myself repeating the Apostles' Creed that I had learned as a young girl:

> I believe in God the Father Almighty, maker of heaven and earth, and in Jesus Christ His only Son our Lord, who was conceived by the Holy Spirit, born of the Virgin Mary, suffered under Pontius Pilate, was crucified, dead, and buried. He descended into hell; the third day he rose again from the dead. He ascended into heaven, and sitteth on the right hand of God the Father

Almighty. From thence he shall come to judge the quick and the dead. I believe in the Holy Spirit; the holy catholic church; the communion of saints; the forgiveness of sins; the resurrection of the body, and the life everlasting. Amen.

This Creed has become my bedrock, the Rock that does not roll. It is my core belief.

We read excerpts from John 14 at many funerals: the part about not letting our hearts be troubled, that Jesus has gone to prepare a place for us, in His Father's house are many mansions, and He will come and take us there (v. 1–4). Jesus answered the protests of Thomas by emphatically stating: "I am the way, the truth and the life. No one comes to the Father except through Me" (v. 6).

There are many who say that Jesus is just "A" way, that there are other ways to God. If this were true, then Jesus is a liar because He said He is the only way. Also, in the Garden of Gethsemane prior to His arrest, He prayed to the Father that if possible, this cup would pass from Him. In other words, if there is another way, please shield me from the cross. There was no other way; He was it! What a cruel, heartless Father if there had been another provision for our sins. The blood of Christ Jesus was required because without the shedding of blood, there is no remission of sin (Heb. 9:22).

Phillip asks Jesus to show them the Father (John 14:8), and Jesus replies that if they have seen Him, they have seen the Father, because He is in the Father and the Father is in Him (v. 9).

Have you heard the phrase, "spitting image?" For instance in the South (where I am from), a son may look so much like his father that someone would say, "Spit right out of his mouth!" Jesus is the "spitting image" of the Father.

In verses 16–17, Jesus promises that He will not leave us as orphans, but He will send another Helper, another one like Him ("spitting image"): "And I will pray the Father, and He will give you another Helper, that He may abide with you forever—the Spirit of truth, whom the world cannot receive, because it neither sees Him nor knows Him; but you know Him, for He dwells with You and will be in you."

Witness Lee puts it concisely: "Just as God is embodied in Christ, so Christ is realized in the wonderful Person of the Holy Spirit. Christ is not separate from God, and the Spirit is not separate from Christ. Christ is God expressed, and the Spirit is Christ realized in reality."[21]

All this set me to thinking about three other profound questions: Who is God the Father? Who is God the Holy Spirit? And who am I?

Chapter Eleven

Who is God, the Father?

THE HOLY BIBLE begins with this statement: "In the beginning God created the heavens and the earth" (Gen. 1:1). There is no detailed explanation telling us who this God is, no adjectives to describe God—He just is. The Hebrew translation here is "Elohim," which is plural. As we read further, there is a reference to the Spirit of God "hovering over the face of the waters" (v. 2). Continuing in verse 3, "Then God *said...*" and we can see the various stages of creation. We know from Scripture in the New Testament that this God Who is speaking is Jesus: "In the beginning was the Word, and the Word was with God, and the Word was God. He was in the beginning with God. All things were made through Him, and without Him nothing was made that was made" (John 1:1–3).

Thus we see that this is a Triune God, operating in three persons: God the Father, God the Son, and God the Holy Spirit. A friend of mine once used an analogy of an egg to explain the Trinity. The egg has three parts: the shell, the white, and the yolk, but it is one egg. Water can also be in three forms: liquid, solid (ice), and gas (steam). An apple has three parts: skin, pulp, and seed.

Being from the South, I especially like Witness Lee's example of the watermelon: "Let me illustrate it in this way: if you buy a watermelon, your intention is to eat and digest this melon. In other words, your intention is to work this melon into you. How can this be done? First, you buy the whole melon; second, you cut it into slices; then, thirdly, before this melon enters your stomach, you chew it until it becomes juice. The sequence is: melon, slices, and finally. juice. Are these three different things or just one? I believe this is the best illustration of the Trinity. Most melons are larger than your stomach. How can you swallow a large melon when your mouth is so small and your throat so slender? Before it can become the proper size for you to eat, it must be cut into slices. Then, once it is eaten, it becomes juice. Are the slices not the melon? And is the juice not the melon? If we say that they are not, we must be most ignorant. The Father is illustrated by the whole melon; the Son by the slices; and finally, the Spirit by the juice...Originally, the melon was on the table, but after being eaten, the melon is in the whole family."[22]

In John 15:1–10, Jesus spoke of being *in* Him and the Father, using the illustration of the vine and the branches, the "abiding." He says that He is the true vine and the Father is the husbandman. When we "abide" (make our habitation) in Him, and He in us, we bear fruit, and that brings glory to the Father. Witness Lee further says: "The main thing in the economy of God is that God intends to work Himself into us. He works Himself into our different parts through His different Persons...in the whole universe God's intention is nothing other than to work Himself into man."[23]

Since Jesus was there at the beginning with God the Father, and God the Holy Spirit, He is an expert witness. He often referred to God as His Father, and our Father. When Jesus was twelve, Mary and Joseph took Him to Jerusalem for the Feast of the Passover. On their way home, they discovered Jesus was missing, and when they frantically returned to Jerusalem, they found Him in the temple, seated among the teachers, listening to them and asking questions. The teachers were impressed. When Mary reprimanded Him, He answered, "Did you not know that I must be about My Father's business?" (Luke 2:49).

Jesus was baptized by John the Baptist in the Jordan River prior to beginning His ministry at the age of thirty. As Jesus came out of the water, the Father said in a voice from heaven: "You are my beloved Son; in You I am well pleased" (Luke 3:22).

The disciples asked Jesus to teach them how to

pray, and He taught them the model prayer, which Christians call "The Lord's Prayer" (Matt. 6:9–13):

> Our Father in heaven, Hallowed be Your name. Your kingdom come. Your will be done on earth as it is in heaven. Give us this day our daily bread, and forgive us our debts, as we forgive our debtors. And do not lead us into temptation, but deliver us from the evil one. For Yours is the kingdom and the power and the glory forever. Amen.

The disciples are to approach God as their Father. Jesus further warns: "For if you forgive men their trespasses, your heavenly Father will also forgive you. But if you do not forgive men their trespasses, neither will your Father forgive your trespasses" (Matt. 6:14). They are to be obedient to their heavenly Father; keep the lines of communication open.

As we look back at the creation story in Genesis 1, we see that God was making a home for His man, and when all was ready, He took the dust of the earth and created His masterpiece (Gen. 2:7). The Message Translation reads: "God spoke: 'Let us make human beings in our image, make them reflecting our nature so they can (take dominion).'"

> God created human beings; he created them godlike, reflecting God's nature. He created them male and female. God blessed them: "Prosper! Reproduce! Fill Earth! Take Charge!"
> —GENESIS 1:26–28

God wanted a family, lots of children, and He gave
Adam and Eve all they needed to accomplish the task.
He wanted intimate relationship, walking with Adam
in the garden in the cool of the day (Gen. 3:8). The only
rule was that Adam and Eve not eat of the tree of the
knowledge of good and evil (Gen. 2:17). Of course, we
know that children do exactly that thing they are told
not to do; Adam and Eve were no different. They ate
the fruit of the forbidden tree, but God, in His grace,
provided a promised remedy. He speaks to Satan, the
tempter: "Because you have done this, you are cursed
more than all cattle, and more than every beast of the
field: On your belly you shall go, and you shall eat dust
all the days of your life. And I will put enmity between
you and the woman, and between your seed and her
Seed; He shall bruise your head, and you shall bruise
His heel" (Gen. 3:14–15, NKJV).

The "Seed of the woman" refers to Father God's son,
Jesus Christ, who was conceived by the Holy Spirit and
born of the Virgin Mary. What wondrous love is this!

If you are a Christian, and even if you're not, you
undoubtedly have either read in the Bible (Exodus) or
seen in the movies the account of Moses, the burning
bush, the ten plagues in Egypt, and the forty-year wilderness journey of the Israelites before entering the
Promised Land. In Chapter 3 we discover God's reply
to a most profound question posed to Him by Moses.

Moses had fled from the wrath of Pharaoh in Egypt,
and is tending the flock of Jethro, his father-in-law,
on the backside of the desert, when he sees a bush

that is burning but not consumed. As he turns aside to investigate, God speaks to him, calling him by name. Moses replies, "Here am I." God then instructs Moses to remove his shoes, for he is standing on holy ground (Ex. 3:1–5).

Then God identifies Himself: "I am the God of your Father—the God of Abraham, the God of Isaac, and the God of Jacob" (v. 6).

God has seen the oppression of His people, and has heard their cries. Now it is time to keep His covenant promise to Abraham: "Know certainly that your descendants will be strangers in a land that is not theirs, and will serve them, and they will afflict them four hundred years. And also the nation whom they serve I will judge; afterward they shall come out with great possessions" (Gen. 15:13–14).

Our God is faithful to keep His covenant; it is time for His children to go home!

> But Moses said to God, "Who am I that I should go to Pharaoh, and that I should bring the children of Israel out of Egypt?"
> —VERSE 11

God does not go into Moses' qualifications for the task, He merely states, ""I will certainly be with you. And this shall be a sign to you that I have sent you: When you have brought the people out of Egypt, you shall serve God on this mountain" (v. 12). Note that God is saying that the fact He is with Moses guarantees success; the outcome is assured. Now we come to the big question in verse 13: "Then Moses said to God, 'Indeed, when I come to the children of Israel and say to them, "The God of your fathers has sent me to you," and they say to me, "What is His name?" what shall I say to them?'"

The Egyptians had many gods, and they all had names, so this was a reasonable question. The Israelites had lived in this culture over four hundred years; they had been slaves and most likely felt forgotten by God. Additionally, your name represents who you are. Basically, Moses is asking God Who He is.

Here is God's awesome answer: "'I AM WHO I AM.' And He said, 'Thus you shall say to the children of Israel, "I AM has sent me to you."'" Moreover God said to Moses, "Thus you shall say to the children of Israel: 'The Lord God of your fathers, the God of Abraham, the God of Isaac, and the God of Jacob, has sent me to you. This is My name forever, and this is My memorial to all generations'" (v. 14–15).

The Christian Life Bible expounds on this: "God is saying, I am self-existent, eternal Jehovah God. I am immutable. I do not change (Mal. 3:6). There are only two ways to change—for better or for worse; God cannot do either, because this would be inconsistent with His absolutely perfect character. He is infallible; He errs not; He is incapable of sin (James 1:13). He is the great I AM."[24]

There are many other names for God, some of which are: Elohim (Powerful God); Jehovah (Self-Existing One); Adonai (Master); El-Elyon (God

Most High); El-Elam (God Everlasting); Jehovah Rohi (My Shepherd); Jehovah Shammach (The Lord Is There); Jehovah Nissi (My Banner); Jehovah Jireh (My Provider); Jehovah Rapha (God Who Heals); El Shaddai (God All Mighty, All Sufficient One); Jehovah Shalom (God of Peace); Jehovah Melek (Lord Is King); Jehovah Tsidkenu (God of Righteousness); Immanuel (God With Us); and Pater (Father). The name Jesus used most was Abba Father, which is the most precious and intimate and means "Daddy God."[25]

If you came from a broken home, or perhaps had a father who was harsh and abusive, it could be difficult to relate to God as Father. In that case, you must use your imagination. Picture what characteristics you think the perfect father would have, how he would treat you, how he would shower his love on you. That is your Abba Father.

I was blessed to have parents who married young and stayed together. When my daddy died in 1978, he had been married to my Mom for forty-four years. I never once heard my daddy say that he loved me. He came from a stern, disciplined, and unemotional family; there were few hugs and kisses. That did not stop my loving him, and I was so proud that he was a Marine in World War II. He volunteered to go, and we did not see him after he left for more than three years. I was in the living room alone, stringing popcorn for our Christmas tree. He was on his way to Camp LeJuene for discharge and had a short layover. I remember hugging him so tight, my arms around his waist, and I was not about to let go. He was hugging me back, and we were laughing and crying at the same time.

Many years later I took some counseling courses and learned that we show our love in different ways. Those who have trouble expressing their love in words, demonstrate it by their actions. My daddy worked very hard to provide for us, and when our nation was attacked, he voluntarily went to war, risking his life to protect not only his family, but his country as well. His actions spoke his love much louder than words!

During my lifetime here on this earth, I have called upon my God in every conceivable situation. He has been and is the God who heals, the God who provides; the God who is there, the God who meets every need, the strong One, the God who is my peace.

It is mind-boggling to know that He is the Great I AM—not I was, or I am going to be, but I AM right now! And He leaves the statement open-ended. Whatever your need is, that is what He is, now. If I'm broke, He says, "I AM your banker." If I'm sick, He says, "I AM your healer." If I'm feeling lonely, He says, "I AM your comforter." If I need direction, He says, "I AM your guide." The supply is endless.

Romans 10:9–10 is often used to lead people to Christ for salvation (NKJV): "If you confess with your mouth the Lord Jesus and believe in your heart that God has raised Him from the dead, you will be saved. For with the heart one believes unto righteousness, and with the mouth confession is made unto salvation." And verse 13 says: "For whoever calls on the *name* of the Lord shall be saved" (emphasis added).

So whatever your situation, there is a name for God on which you can call, and you will be delivered, rescued and saved. That is good news!

The Book of Job was written in B.C. 1843–1703 before the law was given to Moses. *Dake's Annotated Reference Bible* says: "[Job]...is a treatise on human sufferings and the effects upon the sufferer and his friends, and reasoning about why these things happen even to the godly of the earth, identify Satan as the author of such misery...and reveal God as the Deliverer of His people when He is called upon to help in time of need."[26]

Job begins with God praising Job, calling him "the greatest of all the people of the East." He got up early every morning to offer burnt offerings on behalf of his children. Satan approaches the Lord, whereupon the Lord asks Satan a question (v. 8): "Have you considered My servant Job, that there is none like him on the earth, a blameless and upright man, one who fears God and shuns evil?"

Satan answers the Lord with more questions (v. 9): "Does Job fear God for nothing? Have You not made a hedge around him, around his household, and around all that he has on every side? You have blessed the work of his hands, and his possessions have increased in the land. But now stretch out Your hand and touch all that he has, and he will surely curse You to Your face!" And the Lord replies: "Behold, all that he has in your power; only do not lay a hand on his person."

Satan immediately begins his attack and for the next thirty-seven chapters; there is a running dialogue between Job and his "miserable comforters" (16:2). Eliphaz claims Job has sinned, Bildad says he should repent, Zophar urges him to reach out to God, and younger Elihu serves a huge helping of condemnation on all of them. Meanwhile, Job is protesting his innocence, even to his wife, who urges him to curse God and die (2:9). Remember, she has lost ten children, her husband has lost everything, and she feels forsaken.

Finally, the Lord has had enough and beginning in Chapter 38:2–18, He poses some questions to Job: "Why do you confuse the issue? Why do you talk without knowing what you're talking about? Pull yourself together, Job! Up on your feet! Stand tall! I have some questions for you and I want some straight answers. Where were you when I created the earth? Tell me, since you know so much! Who decided on its size?...And who took charge of the ocean when it gushed forth like a baby from the womb? That was me! ... And have you ever ordered Morning, 'Get up!'...Have you ever gotten to the true bottom of things, explored the labyrinthine caves of deep ocean?...Do you know the first thing about death?...And do you have any idea how large this earth is?" (THE MESSAGE)

Continuing in Chapter 39:1–26, "Do you know the month when mountain goats give birth? ...Who do you think set the wild donkey free, opened the corral gates and let him go?...Will the wild buffalo condescend to serve you, volunteer to spend the night in your barn?...

Was it through your know how that the hawk learned to fly?"

And concluding His questioning (Job 40:1–5): "God then confronts Job directly: 'Now what do you have to say for yourself? Are you going to haul me, the Mighty One, into court and press charges?' Job answered God, saying: 'I'm speechless, in awe—words fail me. I should never have opened my mouth! I've talked too much, way too much. I'm ready to shut up and listen.'"

God has a second set of questions for Job (v. 6–9): "I have some more questions for you, and I want straight answers. Do you presume to tell me what I'm doing wrong? Are you calling me a sinner so you can be a saint? Do you have an arm like my arm? Can you shout out in thunder the way I can?"

Chapter 41:1–11 reads: "Or can you pull in the sea beast Leviathan, with fly rod and stuff him in your creel?...If you can't hold our own against his glowering visage, how, then, do you expect to stand up to me? Who could confront me and get by with it? I'm in charge of all this—I run this universe!"

Job's story concludes in Chapter 42, with Job's repentance and worship. We see Father God as patient, merciful, gracious and generous, bringing reconciliation and restoration.

Job answered God: "I'm convinced You can do anything and everything. Nothing and no one can upset your plans. You asked, 'Who is this muddying the water, ignorantly confusing the issue, second-guessing my purposes?' I admit it. I was the one. I babbled on about things far beyond me, made small talk about wonders way over my head. You told me, 'Listen, and let me do the talking. Let me ask the questions. You give the answers.' I admit I once lived by rumors of you; now I have it all firsthand—from my own eyes and ears! I'm sorry—forgive me. I'll never do that again, I promise! I'll never again live on crusts of hearsay, crumbs of rumor" (v. 1–6).

In the final verses (7–17), God reprimands Job's companions and orders them to sacrifice burnt offerings. He says that His friend, Job, would pray for them and He would accept Job's prayer. After Job interceded for his friends, God restored his fortune, and then doubled it! God blessed Job's later life even more than his earlier life. He lived another 140 years and then he died—an old man, a full life.

Job's experience teaches us the balance between the incredible, awesome power of God and His tender compassion for His man. As frail human beings, we would be prone to think that our God fell into Satan's trap, and Job was set up to lose. But God had other plans for Job; he was set up for promotion. At the end of his test, he did not just have a relationship based on "hearsay," but a personal, intimate relationship based on experience. He knew that he loved and served a "beyond" God.

The Student Bible makes this comment with reference to Exodus 34:6–7: "Capsule Description: The self-description of God found in these two verses become for the Jews a profound summary of God's nature. The

Old Testament quotes or alludes to this passage more than any other: 'And he passed in front of Moses, proclaiming, "The LORD, the LORD, the compassionate and gracious God, slow to anger, abounding in love and faithfulness, maintaining love to thousands, and forgiving wickedness, rebellion and sin."'[27]

A young male student was commiserating with other students about his urgent need to get an appointment with the president of the college. Immediately, a pretty female student took him by the hand and said, "Come with me!" She marched him to the president's office, gently knocked on the door, opened it, and said, "Hi, Daddy. I want you to meet my new friend." She was the child of the "king" and did not need an appointment; also, she was welcome to bring her friend. She knew her "Daddy" loved her, and had the authority to meet not only her needs, but those of her friend.

It really is "who" you know. Just ask Job!

Chapter Twelve

Who is the Holy Spirit?

OD WALFORD SAYS, "A man with an experience is never at the mercy of a man with an
argument."[28]

My encounter with the Holy Spirit occurred at St.
Andrew United Methodist Church in College Park,
Georgia, in May 1975. Our church was holding a Lay
Witness Mission. Our goddaughter had come to live
with us while her parents were going through a divorce.
She had upset my neat little world, and I was questioning my faith. After group sessions, the altar was
open for prayer. I went down and prayed, "God, if You
are real, show me, or I'm getting out of Your church. I
can't cope!" I heard God speaking to my heart, "When
in your life have things not worked out for you?" Then
my life paraded across my mind, and I knew He had

been there all the time. I felt His Spirit bubbling inside of me, starting with my toes and coming up to the top of my head. I knew He was real, and that He loved me.

As I departed the church, I stopped at the book table and picked up a copy of *On Tiptoe With Joy*, by John T. Seamands, which the leader in our group session had recommended. As I stepped into the night air, everything was bright and beautiful. Stars were shining and everything was right in my world. I felt like I was wearing new glasses. When I came home, the family was watching television and I wondered how they could be so calm and ordinary, because I was not! They all went to bed and I waited for my goddaughter, who was on a date. I started to read the book, and it said that the disciples were not drunk, it was only nine o'clock in the morning, but they had been filled with the Holy Spirit, just as the Prophet Joel had prophesied. I slapped my hand on the page and said, "That's what happened to me! I've been filled with the Holy Spirit!" I have not been the same since. I know the Holy Spirit, personally; He has made Father God and my Lord Jesus more intimate to me. He is my teacher, guide, energizer, compass, rudder, comforter, and friend. I did not just receive an "experience" or a "blessing" or an "it," but the Holy Spirit, the Third Person of the Godhead! He lives in me, and I have His Word that He "will never leave me, nor forsake me" (Heb. 13:5).

He was there in the beginning, at the time of creation. Genesis 1:1–2 reads: "First this: God created the Heavens and Earth—all you see, all you don't see.

Earth was a soup of nothingness, a bottomless empti-
ness…God's Spirit brooded like a bird above the watery
abyss" (THE MESSAGE).

Throughout the Old Testament, the Holy Spirit is at
work. He speaks through the mouths of the prophets,
and He gave King Saul, the first king of Israel, a new
heart. Samuel had come to anoint Saul, and Samuel
prophesied to Saul: "Then the Spirit of the Lord will
come upon you, and you will prophesy with them
and be turned into another man. And let it be, when
these signs come to you, that you do as the occasion
demands; for God is with you…So it was when he
turned his back to go from Samuel, that God gave him
another heart; and all those signs came to pass that
day. When they came there to the hill, there was a
group of prophets to meet him; then the Spirit of God
came upon him, and he prophesied among them" (1
Sam. 10:6–7, 9).

We see that in the Old Testament days the Holy
Spirit fell on certain individuals, but a day was coming
when He would come upon *all* flesh, all those who
would receive Him. Joel prophesied: "And it shall come
to pass afterward that I will pour out My Spirit on
all flesh; your sons and your daughters shall prophesy,
your old men shall dream dreams, your young men
shall see visions. And also on My menservants and on
My maidservants I will pour out My Spirit in those
days" (Joel 2:28–29).

In the beginning of the New Testament, the Holy

Spirit came to divide time in half—B.C. (before Christ) and A.D. (anno domini, after Christ).

"Now the birth of Jesus was as follows: After His mother Mary was betrothed to Joseph, before they came together, she was found with child of the Holy Spirit" (Matt. 1:18). The angel told Joseph not to be afraid to take Mary as his wife, "for that which is conceived in her is of the Holy Spirit" (v. 20). This is Joseph's side of the story, and in Luke 1:26–39, we read it from Mary's viewpoint.

The angel Gabriel announces that she has been chosen to bear the Messiah, and in verse 35, He says: "The Holy Spirit will come upon you, and the power of the Highest will overshadow you; therefore, also, that Holy One Who is to be born will be called the Son of God. After Jesus had been circumcised and the days of Mary's purification were ended, Mary and Joseph took Jesus to the temple where He was presented, and they made a sacrifice for their male child. Simeon was there and he recognized that this Baby Jesus was the Messiah. And behold, there was a man in Jerusalem whose name was Simeon, and this man was just and devout, waiting for the Consolation of Israel, and the Holy Spirit was upon him. And it had been revealed to him by the Holy Spirit that he would not see death before he had seen the Lord's Christ. So he came by the Spirit into the temple. And when the parents brought in the Child Jesus, to do for Him according to the custom of the law, he took Him up in his arms and blessed God and said: Lord, now You are letting

Your servant depart in peace, according to Your word" (Luke 2:25–29).

When Jesus, at age thirty was baptized by John the Baptist in the Jordan River, the Bible records a theophany, which is a manifestation of a deity, according to *Merriam–Webster.*

> When all the people were baptized, it came to pass that Jesus also was baptized, and while He prayed, the heaven was opened. And the Holy Spirit descended in bodily form like a dove upon Him, and a voice came from heaven which said: "You are my beloved Son; in you I am well pleased."
>
> —LUKE 3:21-22, NKJV

In this account we see present the Three Persons of the Godhead: Father, Son and Holy Spirit.

Immediately after Jesus' baptism, we read: "Then Jesus, being filled with the Holy Spirit, returned from the Jordan and was led by the Spirit into the wilderness, being tempted for forty days by the devil" (Luke 4:1, NKJV). Jesus did not begin His ministry until He was filled with the power of the Holy Spirit. As followers of Christ, we have this same charge.

Billy Graham, one of the greatest evangelists the world has ever known, in his sermon entitled "How to Be Filled with the Spirit," said: "The very fact that some of us believe one thing and some another does not do away with the fact that God says, 'Be ye filled with the Holy Spirit' (Eph. 5:18). I believe this is the greatest need of the church of Jesus Christ today."[29]

Jesus walked with the disciples for forty days after His resurrection; "speaking of the things pertaining to the kingdom of God" (Acts 1:3). He is ready to pass on to them this same power of the Holy Spirit. Continuing in verses 4–5, and 8: "And being assembled together with them, He commanded them that not to depart from Jerusalem, but to wait for the Promise of the Father, 'which,' He said, 'you have heard from me; for John truly baptized with water; but you shall be baptized with the Holy Spirit not many days from now... But you shall receive power when the Holy Spirit has come upon you; and you shall be witnesses for Me in Jerusalem, and in all Judea and Samaria and to the end of the earth.'"

Jesus is telling them not to rush off and start saving the world, but to wait for the power of the Holy Spirit. In today's vernacular we would say, "Don't rush off and start forming committees!" (The definition of a donkey is that it is a horse formed by a committee.)

The *Christian Life Bible* says: "'Parakletos' is the Greek word used four times in the Book of John, and is translated 'Helper.' The word means 'one called alongside.'"[30]

Jesus reminds them of the His previous Promise to them. This is a capital "P" Promise—the Holy Spirit Himself, and all this entails.

> And I (Jesus) will pray the Father, and He will
> give you another Helper, that He may abide

with you forever—the Spirit of Truth, whom the world cannot receive, because it neither sees Him nor knows Him; but you know Him, for He dwells with you and will be in you. I will not leave you orphans; I will come to you...But the Helper, the Holy Spirit, whom the Father will send in My name, He will teach you all things, and bring to your remembrance all things that I said to you.

—JOHN 14:16–18

Jesus goes into more detail concerning the work of the Holy Spirit in John 16:7–15: "Nevertheless I tell you the truth." Let's stop here for a moment. Whenever you see "nevertheless" in the Bible, substitute "always the more." It is a clue that God is up to something more than you can imagine. He is taking you "beyond!"

To continue: "It is to your advantage that I go away; for if I do not go away, the Helper will not come to you; but if I depart, I will send Him to you" (v. 7).

Do you get the picture of "tag team?" Jesus finishes His work on earth, ascends into heaven, sprinkles His blood on the mercy seat, and tags the Holy Spirit. It's His turn on earth, as Jesus takes His place at the right hand of the Father as our High Priest and Intercessor.

In John 16, Jesus gives the Holy Spirit's job description: He will convict of sin, of righteousness, and of judgment; He will guide you into all truth; He will show you things to come; He will glorify Christ; and He will take the things of Christ, and show it to you. Jesus gave this further word of encouragement to His disciples: "If you then, being evil, know how to give good gifts to your children how much more will your heavenly Father give the Holy Spirit to those who ask Him!" (Luke 11:13, NKJV).

The Holy Spirit will never burst in uninvited; He is a Gentleman of the Highest Order! Your free will shall not be violated, but He yearns for your invitation to take residence in your heart and He will persistently knock.

The Holy Spirit began His ministry of evangelizing the world and guiding the believers on the Day of Pentecost. The followers of Christ had obediently gathered together in Jerusalem, waiting for the Promised Holy Spirit. Acts 2:1–4 describes the scene (NKJV): "When the Day of Pentecost had fully come, they were all with one accord in one place. And suddenly there came a sound from heaven, as of a rushing mighty wind, and it filled the whole house where they were sitting. Then there appeared unto them divided tongues, as of fire, and one sat upon each of them. And they were all filled with the Holy Spirit and began to speak with other tongues as the Spirit gave them utterance."

Peter went out and began preaching in the street in the power of the Holy Spirit, "and that day about three thousand souls were added to them" (Acts 2:41). Jesus had said: "Most assuredly, I say to you, he who believes in Me, the works that I do he will do also; and greater works than these he will do, because I go to my Father" (John 14:12).

We know that Jesus did great and mighty works, such

as raising the dead, healing the sick, setting people free from demons, turning water into wine, stilling storms, and walking on water. But all His divinity was contained in one human body, making His scope limited. The Holy Spirit comes into the hearts of all believers, so in effect He multiplies Jesus and His outreach.

Surely the greatest miracle is the salvation of a soul—regeneration of the spirit, being "born again." Peter launched the "greater works" on the Day of Pentecost, when those three thousand souls were added to the kingdom. We have recorded from Acts to Revelation the mighty exploits of the followers of Christ, as they fulfilled their destinies, just as Jesus foretold; they were given the "right to become" (John 1:12), just as He promised.

> For we are His workmanship, created in Christ Jesus for good works, which God prepared beforehand that we should walk in them.
> —Ephesians 2:10

Father God had plans for us before we were born, before we were a twinkle in our earthly father's eyes. It follows that the Helper will assist us in successfully completing our assignments. He gives us spiritual gifts: "There are diversities of gifts, but the same Spirit. There are diversities of ministries, but the same Lord. And there are diversities of activities, but it is the same God who works all in all. But the manifestation of the Spirit is given to each one for the profit of all; for to one is given the word of wisdom through the Spirit, to another the word of knowledge through the same Spirit, to another faith by the same Spirit, to another gifts of healings by the same Spirit, to another the working of miracles, to another prophecy, to another discerning spirits, to another different kinds of tongues, to another the interpretation of tongues. But the one and same Spirit works all these things, distributing to each one individually as He wills" (1 Cor. 12:4–11, NKJV).

We cannot earn any of these gifts by doing good works or keeping the commandments. It is very simple: A gift is a gift. The Holy Spirit dispenses the gifts as they are needed to build the Body of Christ. There are arguments as to which is the best gift. It seems to me that it is the one that is needed at the time.

During my walk with the Lord, I have seen many healings, including my own. The Holy Spirit has also given me the gift of faith during some difficult times. I would call that when your "knower knows," enabling you to stand until the answer to your prayer is manifested, even if it takes thirty years!

There are no small things in God's kingdom and everything that concerns us concerns Him. I had lost two tickets to a concert, and all my frantic searching was in vain. Finally, I asked the Lord to give me the gift of knowledge. Where are those tickets? (Why do we pray last, instead of first?) I could see in my mind's eye a small trash can in the basement, and the two tickets on top of discarded papers. Sure enough, they were there, and I had a wonderful time at the concert.

Our Lord does not waste anything, as He gave me another testimony of His lavish love!

Not only does the Holy Spirit give gifts, but He produces fruit in Christ's followers: "But the fruit of the Spirit is love, joy, peace, longsuffering, kindness, goodness, faithfulness, gentleness, self-control" (Gal. 5:22, NKJV).

As we yield to the Holy Spirit, He will transform us into the image of Christ so that we, too, will be fruit-bearers in the Kingdom.

We have sonship with the Father through the Holy Spirit; we have been adopted into the family of God. In biblical days a child had no right to address his adoptive father as "Abba, Father," meaning "my Daddy," until the papers were signed and sealed. The tutor would present the adoptive child to his new Daddy. God's Word says that we are sealed: "In Him you also trusted, after you heard the word of truth, the gospel of your salvation, in whom also, having believed, you were sealed with the Holy Spirit of promise, who is the guarantee of our inheritance until the redemption of the purchased possession (that's you and me), to the praise of His glory" (Eph. 1:13–14, NKJV).

The Holy Spirit is our tutor, teaching us about Christ, and presenting us to the Father; He is our "guarantee," our down payment, the earnest money. We have His Word: "For as many as are led by the Spirit of God, these are the sons of God. For you did not receive the spirit of bondage again to fear, but you received the Spirit of adoption by whom we cry out, 'Abba, Father.'

The Spirit Himself bears witness with our spirit that we are children of God, and if children, then heirs—heirs of God and joint heirs with Christ, if indeed we suffer with Him, that we may also be glorified together" (Rom. 8:14–17, NKJV).

There seems to be "a fly in the ointment" here. As believers we have been adopted into the family of God, we are promised an inheritance as a joint-heir with Christ, and one day we will be glorified with Him, BUT, it is "if indeed we suffer with Him." Jesus told us, "In the world you shall have tribulation: but be of good cheer; I have overcome the world" (John 16:33). Suffering is indeed no fun at all, but it is not wasted. The Holy Spirit uses these testing times to build our character, to make us more like Jesus. Just as an oyster when it is irritated brings forth a pearl, so our Lord is making "pearls" of us. It is significant that the gates of heaven are formed of pearl—the suffering of the saints.

The Holy Spirit is also referred to in Scripture as the "Comforter": "He shall give you another Comforter, that he may abide with you forever" (John 14:16, KJV); "The Comforter, which is the Holy Ghost" (14:26, KJV); "When the Comforter is come" (15:26, KJV).

David Wilkerson writes: "'Comforter' means one who soothes in a time of pain or grief—one who eases pain and sorrow…I like the following definition from the Greek: 'One who lays you down on a warm bed of safety.' During the cold, dark night of your soul, the Holy Spirit lays you down on the soft bed of his comfort, soothing you tenderly…His comfort to you is contained in two simple phrases. You are loved. And you are leaving."[31]

Prayer is our line of communication as we talk and listen to God, but many times we are perplexed and confused. In steps the Holy Spirit, our Helper: "Likewise, the Spirit also helps us in our weaknesses. for we do not know what we should pray for as we ought, but the Spirit Himself makes intercession for us with groanings which cannot be uttered. Now He who searches the hearts knows what the mind of the Spirit is, because He makes intercession for the saints according to the will of God" (Rom. 8:26–27, NKJV).

The Holy Spirit locks our spirits into the will of God, making our prayers effectual and fervent, thereby accomplishing much (James 5:16). The Message translation renders these prayers as "a powerful force to be reckoned with!" But the cherry on the cake is in Romans 8:28: "And we know that all things work together for good to those who love God, to those who are the called according to His purpose."

We know that all things in our world are not good; that bad things happen to good people. Our Lord says what He means, and He means what He says, and He says He will work *all* things together for our good. "All" means everything, the entire thing with nothing omitted. The Holy Spirit takes our tests and transforms them into testimonies; He takes our messes and makes them messages. Everything the Divine touches turns into gold. It may not seem good at the beginning, but it is when He finishes.

Jesus gives a frightening warning concerning the Holy Spirit in Matthew 12:32–33 (Christians call it "The Unpardonable Sin," NKJV): "Therefore I say to you, every sin and blasphemy will be forgiven men, but the blasphemy against the Spirit will not be forgiven men. Anyone who speaks a word against the Son of Man, it will be forgiven him; but whoever speaks against the Holy Spirit, it will not be forgiven him, either in this age or in the age to come."

Jesus had healed a man who was demon-possessed, blind and mute. The Pharisees said that Jesus accomplished this miracle through the power of Satan. Jesus now draws a line in the sand, and gives them a choice to be either for Him or against Him. He is in effect saying, "You can pick on Me, but you better keep your mouth shut about the Holy Spirit! When you do that, you've gone too far!"

Vine's Expository Dictionary explains: "...that anyone, with the evidence of the Lord's power before his eyes, should declare it to be Satanic, exhibited a condition of heart beyond Divine illumination and therefore hopeless. Divine forgiveness would be inconsistent with the moral nature of God. As to the Son of Man, in his state of humiliation, there might be misunderstanding, but not so with the Holy Spirit's power demonstrated."[32]

If you think you have committed the unpardonable sin and are doomed to hell, you can relax. The very fact that you are concerned is evidence that you care, and: "There is therefore *now* no condemnation to those who are in Christ Jesus, who do not walk according to the flesh, but according to the Spirit" (Rom, 8:1, NKJV, emphasis added).

There is a tender scene in the movie *Jerry Maguire*. In the elevator a deaf couple looks adoringly at each other, and the deaf man "signs" a message to the woman; she leans her head against his chest in sweet response. Jerry turns to his girlfriend and asks what the man has said. She replies, "You complete me." You probably say to yourself, "Isn't that precious!" In reality, it is not precious, because this couple is being positioned for failure. No human being can fully meet the needs or desires of another; no human being can "complete" another.

That is the task of the Holy Spirit!

Chapter Thirteen

Who am I?

LORETTA YOUNG WAS a beautiful, talented actress who appeared both in movies and on television. She had her own show on television from 1953 through 1963. The set was a fashionably decorated parlor, and the camera would focus on a door. It would open and she would sweep into the room adorned in an elegant gown. She would then very sweetly inform her audience about the story that was to follow. Of course, she always played the lead.

In one episode she was writing a research paper, which required her to interview people to gain insight as to how they viewed themselves, their self esteem. Time was of the essence and she was searching for a concise formula. She had the brilliant idea of asking the people to answer one question with three short statements. The question was "Who are you?"

The majority answered first with their profession, such as, "I am a teacher." Second might be their marital status, and third could be their religious status, such as, "I am Catholic." The answers would vary as to being a father, mother, or the number of children. Very few answered the first statement with their name. The conclusion was that most people identify themselves by what they do.

My name is Betty June Terry Smith. The "Betty" came from the nickname for my great-grandmother. The "June" was because I was born in June, and my mother thought that would be appropriate. My father's surname was "Terry" and I married into the "Smith" family. All of this was a part of God's plan.

After my husband left, I was searching the Word for hope, and the Lord gave me Isaiah 54 as my very own. In verse 5, He promised to be my husband! I would laughingly tell my friends that I was Mrs. Jesus! Just as Ruth in the Old Testament married Boaz, and became the richest woman in town, I was the bride of Jesus, and I was the richest woman in the world!

> He (God) gives to all life, breath, and all things. And He has made from one blood every nation of men to dwell on all the face of the earth, and has determined their pre-appointed times and the boundaries of their dwellings, so that they should seek the Lord...for in Him we live and

move and have our being...For we are also His offspring.

—ACTS 17:25–28, NKJV

Warren Buffett, one of the richest men in the world and a shrewd investor, said when interviewed that he had won the "ovarian lottery," because he had been born in America. He didn't win any lottery, and neither did you nor I, because it was God who chose where and when we would be born, our human families. We had nothing to do with it!

Our Father God further says in Jeremiah 29:11: "For I know the thoughts that I think toward you, says the Lord, thoughts of peace and not of evil, to give you a future and a hope" (NKJV). And here is God boasting: "For we are His workmanship, created in Christ Jesus unto good works, which God prepared beforehand that we should walk in them" (Eph. 2:10, NKJV).

God has a plan, and as His "workmanship," we play a major role.

> But when the fullness of time had come, God sent forth His Son, born of a woman, born under the law, to redeem those who were under the law, that we might receive the adoption as sons. And because you are sons, God has sent forth the Spirit of His Son into your hearts, crying out 'Abba, Father!' (That means Daddy God.) Therefore you are no longer a slave but a son, and if a son, then an heir of God through Christ.
>
> —GALATIANS 4:4–7, NKJV

We are Christ's family, His heirs:

> In Christ's family there can be no division into Jew and non-Jew, slave and free, male and female. Among us you are all equal. That is, we are all in a common relationship with Jesus Christ. Also, since you are Christ's family, then you are Abraham's famous descendant, heirs according to the covenant promises.
> —GALATIANS 3:28–29, THE MESSAGE

King David asked God this question: "Lord, what is man, that You take knowledge of him? Or the son of man, that You are mindful of him?" (Ps. 144:3, NKJV).

Let's get a bit more fundamental and go back to the beginning of our Bible, the Book of Genesis. What do we learn about "man?" "In the beginning God" created a home for His man; it took five days and each day was "good." But what God did on the sixth day was "very good!"

> Then God said, "Let us make man in Our image, according to Our likeness; let them have dominion . . . over every living thing that moves on the earth"
> —GENESIS 1:26, 28, NKJV

We are made in the image of God! Our God is a Triune God, which includes the Father, the Son, and the Holy Spirit; He is one God in Three Persons. Likewise, we are each one person, comprised of three parts. We have a body, a soul and a spirit. Our soul consists of the mind, will and emotions; and our spirit has a conscience and intuition, and it is through our spirit that we have fellowship with God.

In 1 Thessalonians 5:23, we read (NKJV): "Now may the God of peace Himself sanctify you completely, and may your whole spirit, soul and body be preserved blameless at the coming of our Lord Jesus Christ."

David reflected in Psalm 8:3–5 (NKJV): "When I consider Your heavens, the work of Your fingers, the moon and the stars, which You have ordained, what is man that You are mindful of him, and the son of man that you visit him? For You have made him a little lower the an the angels, and You have crowned him with glory and honor."

David goes on to say in Psalm 139 that the Lord has a perfect knowledge of man; He knows when we sit down or stand up, the words on our tongues; He is behind and before us, and His hand is upon us (v. 1–6). There is no place we can go to flee from His Spirit—neither heaven nor hell, nor darkness nor night (v. 7–12). Verses 13–16 read: "For You formed my inward parts; You covered me in my mother's womb. I will praise You, for I am fearfully and wonderfully made; marvelous are Your works, and that my soul knows very well. My frame was not hidden from You when I was made in secret, and skillfully wrought in the lowest parts of the earth; Your eyes saw my substance, being yet unformed. And in Your book they were all written, the days fashioned for me, when as yet there were none of them. How precious are Your thoughts to me, O God!"

And that's not all, because He knows also the numbers of hairs on our heads (Matt. 10:30), and He keeps our tears in a bottle (Ps. 56:8). Our names are engraved on the palms of His hands (Isa. 49:16), like when we had sweethearts in school. I would draw a cross and put: B.T. + B.S. That meant that Betty Terry loves Bob Smith. Jesus Christ loves me (and you)! I heard once that if God had a refrigerator, your picture would be on it!

If I were kidnapped, what would be the cost of my redemption? Psalm 49:6–8 has the answer (NKJV): "Those who trust in their wealth and boast in the multitude of their riches, none of them can by any means redeem his brother, nor give to God a ransom for him— For the redemption of their souls is costly."

Through the sin of Adam and Eve in the Garden of Eden, the entire human race inherited that original sin and were "kidnapped" by Satan. The only one who could pay the price was God's only Son, our Lord Jesus Christ, through His sacrifice on the cross. All the gold and silver in the world cannot set one person free. The redemption of our souls is indeed "costly," and are we not glad we have an Elder Brother Who loved us enough to leave a throne in glory to come to earth and rescue His brothers and sisters! (1 Peter 1: 18–19) That is "Amazing Grace!"

Everyone wants to be accepted; rejection wounds the spirit. For instance, looking for a job is a bummer, because you are making yourself vulnerable—a target for rejection. It takes a special calling to be a sales person; you hear "no" many times more than "yes." And the boy-girl thing! It is painful to remember the times you were dumped, but how great the joy of being accepted.

> Blessed be the God and Father of our Lord Jesus Christ, Who has blessed us with every spiritual blessing in the heavenly places in Christ...to the praise of the glory of His grace, by which He made us accepted in the Beloved.
> —EPHESIANS 1:3, 6, NKJV

Jesus invites us to abide (remain, inhabit, continue, tarry) in Him. When we accept this invitation, we glorify the Father, bear much fruit, and become His disciples. Another benefit is that our prayers are more powerful (John 15:1–17). Jesus, in His Priestly prayer prior to His arrest in the Garden of Gethsemane, asks the Father: "That they all may be one as You Father, are in Me, and I in You; that they also may be one in Us, that the world may believe that You sent Me, and the glory which You gave Me I have given them, that they may be one, just as We are one; I in them, and You in Me; that they may be made perfect (mature) in one, and that the world may know that You have sent Me, and have loved them as You have loved Me" (John 17:21–23, NKJV).

That, my friends, is shouting ground! Our Heavenly Father loves us just as much as He loves His Son!

Paul says in 1 Corinthians 4:7 (NKJV): "We have this treasure in earthen vessels, that the excellence of the power may be of God and not of us." He continues this theme in 2 Timothy 2:20–21: "But in a great house there are not only vessels of gold and silver, but also of wood and clay, some for honor and some for dishonor. Therefore if anyone cleanses himself from the latter, he will be a vessel of honor, sanctified and useful for the Master, prepared for every good work."

We are called to be "containers" that God can fill with Himself, for He is the treasure. In today's economy, we would be the Styrofoam cups, which are common, ordinary and disposable. The important thing is what is in the container. Our God uses the ordinary to do extra-ordinary things in His Kingdom. As we are transformed into "vessels of honor," He gets the glory. All as it should be.

Paul wrote to the Corinthians, "Your body is the temple of the Holy Spirit" (1 Cor. 6:19). Christ said He would "build" His church (Matt. 16:16–18). Every part is "fitted together" and, therefore, important. The roof of the temple is not more important than the basement; the head of the body is not more important than the neck, for it takes the neck to turn the head! We all matter to God; there are no small things in His kingdom.

Jesus came into my heart when I was thirteen years old, but I remained a "baby" Christian until I was filled with the Holy Spirit in May 1975. What happened to me is described in 2 Corinthians 5:17 (NKJV):

"Therefore, if anyone is in Christ, he is a new creation; old things have passed away; behold, all things have become new."

The phrase "new creation" means a new "species of being." I looked the same on the outside, but inside I was totally different. I had been "born again!" I was "in the world" but not "of it." I was a Kingdom kid, and I had an unquenchable thirst for God's Word. I wanted to "know (have an intimate relationship with) my Father, and Jesus Christ, Whom He had sent" (John 17:3). The Holy Spirit was my Helper, and I wanted Him to use me, to teach me, and guide me. I was an excited and enthusiastic convert. The most precious thing was that this experience did not diminish with time, but accelerated. There have been valleys, of course, but these valleys have their potential, their reward. Jesus promises that He will never leave or forsake us (Matt. 28:20), and when He brings us to it, He takes us through it, because He "works all things together for good to those who love God, to those who are the called according to His purpose" (Rom. 8:28).

There was a little boy whose eternal optimism irked those around him. His parents thought this was abnormal and decided to have him evaluated. The doctor ran a test. He filled a room with manure, gave the boy a shovel, and told him to start digging. He thought the boy would tire of this "stinking" assignment, but the boy grabbed the shovel and started to dig frantically, declaring "There has to be a horse in here somewhere!"

Perhaps the definition of a Christian should include "eternal optimists who carry shovels."

Abraham was described as a "friend of God"(2 Chron. 20:7); David was a "man after God's own heart" (1 Sam. 13:14); and Enoch "walked with God" (Gen. 5:22). When Satan came to present himself to the Lord, the Lord proudly asked: "Have you considered my servant Job, that there is none like him on the earth, a blameless and upright man, one who fears God and shuns evil?" (Job 1:8, NKJV).

In order to answer the question, "Who Am I," we have sought God's Word and explored personal experiences, which are excellent sources, but perhaps a more probing question should be posed, such as:

What Were You Thinking?

What were You thinking, Lord, when You made
the rose?
    From bud to full bloom in beauty it unfolds.
    What were You thinking, Lord, when You
made the tree—
    From acorn to sapling to spreading canopy?
    I look all around me at Your creation,
    The glory of Your people in every nation.
    I see Your blessings of mercy and grace
    Poured out lavishly on every race.
    And I stop and wonder and have to ask,
    What were You thinking, Lord, when You
made me?
    Am I delicate as a rose, or mighty as a tree?
    No, Lord, I'm just me.
    But I'm an original—one of a kind,
    And I love You, Lord, with all my heart, soul,
and mind!

—BETTY SMITH, 1975

Conclusion

WHEN JESUS TOLD His disciples they were going to the "other side" (Mark 4:35), He did not mean just to the other side of the lake. He would take them much farther than that because there was a world that needed to hear the Good News; they were to be His ambassadors. He was taking them "beyond."

When the Lord gave me Isaiah 54 and said He would be my husband, my eyes jumped to verse 4 and on to the end of the chapter. I failed to take in the first three verses, wherein He told me to "enlarge" the place of my tent, to "stretch out" the curtains of my dwelling, and to "strengthen" my stakes. I was going to "expand" to the right and to the left. My life was not over; I was entering into a new season! He was taking me "beyond" the heartache and pain.

I never dreamed I would be a "traveling woman!" I had been in Georgia all my life, and did not cross the state line until my honeymoon, when my husband took me to Florida!

I pray that you, dear reader, have enjoyed our travels "beyond," as we returned to Reynosa, Mexico with three generations, and that the experiences of various "Podiums, Places and People" brought you pleasure, as well as insight.

I do hope you had fun at the retreat in lovely Jefferson, Georgia, and that the teachings touched your heart. I wish you had been there in person! I fervently desire that "My Eventful Day" has inspired you to believe in the power of intercessory prayer.

I'm so glad you came to Italy with my family and me, where history is still alive and celebrated. The enemy attempted to steal that dream trip from me through a hit-and-run driver, but my Lord intervened and took me "beyond" my boundaries to share treasures with my family, and you.

I am delighted that we concluded our journey at my beloved Indian Springs and Camp Meeting. It truly is holy ground, and I pray you could sense that through these pages. It is the best place to find answers to the questions in the "corners of your minds."

I began this book with this question: Is that all there is? I believe we have the answer.

No, emphatically *no!* That is not all there is! We serve a "Beyond God!"

There is more—so much more!

Not the end!

Notes

Chapter 4
You Can Be Faith-Full in a Faith-Less
World: Building Your Faith God's Way

1. *Vine's Expository Dictionary of New Testament Words* (McLean,. VA: MacDonald Publishing Company, Inc.).

2. Robert E. Coleman, "The Spirit and the Word," 4th ed. (Christian Outreach, Wilmore, KY, 1998), 40.

3. Helen Roseveare, "Living Faith," (Minneapolis, MN: Bethany House Publishers, 1980), 20.

4. Leo Buscaglia, "God Quotes and Sayings," http://www.quotegarden.com/gd/html, (accessed 2/18/11).

Chapter 5
The Power of a Virtuous Woman:
Accessing the Goodness of God

5. *Dake's Annotated Reference Bible* (Lawrenceville, GA: Dake Bible Sales, Inc., 1968), 174.

6. *Vine's Expository Dictionary of New Testament Words,* 1212.

7. Julian of Norwich, "Revelations of Divine Love," (Great Britain, Bungay, Suffolk: The Chaucer Press, Ltd., 1966; Reprint Penguin Books, 1982), 70.

Chapter 6
Don't Hang in There—Stand on the Promises of God:
Applying the Promises of God

8. Ruth Bell Graham, "Prodigals and Those Who Love Them." (Colorado Springs, CO: Focus on the Family, 1991), 150.

9. Web site: www.goodreads.com/author/quotes/838305_Mother_Te (accessed 2/28/11).

10. R. Kelso Carter, "Standing on the Promises," (St. Louis, MO: Chalice Press, 1995).

11. Web site: http://healingandrevival.com/BioRKCarter.htm (accessed 4/10/10).

Chapter 7
My Eventful Day

12. *Vine's Expository Dictionary of New Testament Words,* 607.

13. Dutch Sheets, "Intercessory Prayer," (Ventura, CA: Regal Books, 1996), 28.

14. Ibid., 104.

15. Witness Lee, "The Economy of God," (Anaheim, CA: Living Stream Ministry, 1968), 67.

16. Dutch Sheets, "Intercessory Prayer," (Ventura, CA: Regal Books, 1996), 31.

Chapter 8
To Italy With Love

17. Alfred A. Knopf, "Venice-Knopf MapGuides," (New York, NY: Borzoi Book, 2009).

18. http://en.wikipedia.org/wiki/David_Michelangelo - 89k (accessed 2/25/11).

19. http://en.wikipedia.org.wiki/Cinque_terre (accessed 3/2/11).

20. http://www.sacred-destinations.com/italy/rome - sistine - chapel (accessed 2/26/11).

Chapter 10
The Most Profound Question(s)

21. Witness Lee, "Economy of God," (Anaheim, CA: Living Stream Ministry, 1968), 14.

Chapter 11
Who is God, the Father?

22. Witness Lee, "Economy of God," Ibid., 46,47

23. Ibid., 43

24. *The Christian Life Bible,* (Nashville, TN, Thomas Nelson Publishers, 1985) 61.

25. Web site: http://www.characterbuildingforfamilies.com/ names.htm (accessed July 9, 2011).

26. *Dake's Annotated Reference Bible* (Lawrenceville, GA: Dake Bible Sales, Inc., 1963), 543.

27. *The Student Bible*, NIV, Notes by Philip Yancey and Tim Stafford. (Grand Rapids, MI: Zondervan Publishing House, 1998) 118.

Chapter 12
Who is the Holy Spirit?

28. Web site: http://www.drleons.com/quotes.htm (accessed 1/14/11).

29. Robert E. Coleman, Ph.D., "The Spirit and the Word," (Wilmore, KY: Christian Outreach, 1998), 16.

30. *The Christian Life Bible*, 1075.

31. David Wilkerson, "You Have a Comforter," (World Challenge Pulpit Series, January 3, 2011).

32. *Vine's Expository Dictionary of New Testament Words,* 134.

About the Author

BETTY T. SMITH is a native Georgian and a retired legal secretary. She has a master's degree in Christian Counseling from Logos Christian College in Jacksonville, Florida. Betty has served on lay witness missions with various denominations. She is the mother of two sons and one daughter and the grandmother of five.

Betty is the author of two earlier books, *Around the World in Seventy Years* and *Nothing Wasted*.

Contact the Author

Website:

www.bettyterrysmith.com

Or e-mail:

betty@bettyterrysmith.com